Pascoe Francis Polkinghorne

List of British Vertebrate Animals

Pascoe Francis Polkinghorne

List of British Vertebrate Animals

ISBN/EAN: 9783337815134

Printed in Europe, USA, Canada, Australia, Japan

Cover: Foto ©ninafisch / pixelio.de

More available books at **www.hansebooks.com**

LIST

OF

BRITISH VERTEBRATE ANIMALS.

BY

FRANCIS P. PASCOE.

LONDON:
TAYLOR AND FRANCIS, RED LION COURT, FLEET STREET.
1885.

PREFACE.

Just fifty years ago the Rev. Leonard Jenyns published a list* of British vertebrate animals,—the first and last, I believe, for few British naturalists care for reptiles and fishes. Birds have many admirers, and for them there is no lack of lists; still, I think, there are many persons interested in the productions of our land and seas to whom this list may be acceptable. I believe it is "down to date," although I have not thought it necessary to follow every change of name on the ground of priority—changes which are "productive of much confusion and unnecessary novelty."

The law of priority is excellent in principle, and has here been generally followed; but its advantages are questionable when it is adopted to discard a name that has been in common use half a century or more for one

---

* 'A Systematic Catalogue of British Vertebrate Animals,' 1835.

disinterred from some forgotten work, perhaps wrongly identified, or for which priority is wrongly claimed.

Looking at classification only as a key to the names of species, it can hardly be too simple provided mere resemblances are not mistaken for affinities. A genetic classification is for the future. For some time to come there is not likely to be any close agreement among naturalists as to the higher divisions of the vertebrate classes; but whether we divide living birds into two orders, like Professor Huxley, or into twenty-six, like Mr. Sclater, there is less diversity as we descend to families and genera. In this list I have followed the system adopted in my 'Zoological Classification.' The only changes made are those replacing the name of Pharyngobranchii by Acrania, and that of Scansores by Coccyges.

In a strictly scientific system according to modern views the Vertebrata would be divided into Acrania and Craniota (without a skull and with a skull), the former including two genera (only one British), the latter all other Vertebrata. Some would add the Ascidians under the collective name of Chordata. Then we have three primary divisions of Vertebrata—fishes and amphibians constituting the Ichthyopsida; reptiles and birds the

Sauropsida; and, thirdly, the Mammals. A tabular view will show these divisions and the pages in this 'List' on which those here adopted may be found:—

> ACRANIA, p. 1.
> CRANIOTA.
> > Ichthyopsida.
> > > *Pisces*, pp. 1–25.
> > > *Amphibia*, p. 26.
> > Sauropsida.
> > > *Reptilia*, pp. 27–28.
> > > *Aves*, pp. 29–65.
> > Mammalia, pp. 65–71.

Going back to what may be called the middle ages of biology, Fleming, in his 'History of British Animals' (1828), describes 61 mammals, 237 birds, 14 reptiles, including amphibians, and 170 fishes. In Jenyns's 'Manual of British Vertebrate Animals' (1835) there are 61 mammals, 312 birds, 7 reptiles, 6 amphibians, and 210 fishes. Both these authors include domestic and extinct species and the greater part of the stragglers then known.

The third edition of Yarrell's 'British Birds' (1856) gave 352, and in the third edition of his 'Fishes' (1859) the editor, Sir J. Richardson, brought the number up to 260 species. Couch, in his 'History of the Fishes of the British Islands' (1867), advanced the number to 294, but then such apocryphal species as *Polyprosopi Rashleighanus* and *macer* are pressed into the list.

With regard to birds in modern times, G. R. Gray, in his British Museum Catalogue (1863), enumerates 401 species—115 indigenous, 84 seasonal, 112 occasional, 72 accidental, 11 introduced, and 7 doubtful. Mr. Harting, in his 'Handbook of British Birds' (1872), divides his work into two parts, viz. (1) " British birds properly so called," and (2) " Rare and accidental visitors." Of the former there are 260, of the latter 135 species; and of these a full account of the place, date of capture, and authority are given.

Mr. Wharton's 'List' (1877) includes all birds " which have at least once, beyond doubt, occurred in a truly wild state within the area of the British Isles." They amount to 379 species. Adopting this view of what constitutes a British bird, the authors of the 'List' of the British Ornithologists' Union (1883) enumerate 376 species, and 76 in addition " not positively authenticated as British."

Two important works, not yet completed, must here be mentioned: one is the fourth edition of Yarrell's 'British Birds,' at first edited by Prof. Newton, but now and for some time past by Mr. Howard Saunders. The second is Mr. F. Day's ' History of British Fishes,' by far the best and most exhaustive account we have of them, and whose synonymy I have generally followed.

It is difficult to draw a satisfactory line between residents and regular visitors and stragglers or accidental visitors. Summarizing this "List" we have 181 indigenous fishes and 62 stragglers, including at least four introduced, = 243. Of amphibians there are 7 species, and of reptiles 9, three of which are stragglers or introduced. Birds comprise 447 species, but only 245 are considered to be indigenous (either as residents or migrants), leaving the large number of 202 as accidental visitors, or, as in two or three instances, having probably escaped from confinement. Of mammals there are 63 species; but of these one has been introduced, and three are of very rare occurrence.

The binomial system of nomenclature was only finally adopted after the publication of the 12th edition of the 'Systema Naturæ' in 1766, and it is only from that date that the modern law of priority begins. An exception seems to have been made of Brisson, whose 'Ornithologie' (1760) has furnished the names of many modern genera taken from the mononyms which, in many instances, he gave to species. The 'Fauna Suecica' (1761) may occasionally be found to throw some light on Linnæus's doubtful species.

In all the later lists several species of the Vertebrata, especially of fishes of the older authors, are reduced, either as being varieties, immature forms, or from one of the sexes having been treated as a distinct species; others are so doubtful that they may be ignored altogether.

The following is a list of the abbreviations:—

Aldr., Aldrovandi.
Bechst., Bechstein.
Bl., Bloch.
Blain., Blainville.
Bleek., Bleeker.
Bodd., Boddaert.
Bon., Bonaparte.
Bonn., Bonnaterre.
Briss., Brisson.
Brün., Brünnich.
Cab., Cabanis.
Cuv., Cuvier.
C. & V., Cuvier and Valenciennes.
Daud., Daudin.
Desf., Desfontaines.
Don., Donovan.
Düb. & Kor., Düben and Koren.
Dum., Duméril.
Euphr., Euphrasen.
Fab., Faber.
Fabr., Fabricius (Otto).
Flem., Fleming.
Forst., Forster.
Geoff., Geoffroy.
G. R. G., George R. Gray.
Gesn., Gesner.
Gld., Gould.
Gm., Gmelin.
Günth., Günther.
Ill., Illiger.
Jacq., Jacquin.
J. & S., Jardine and Selby.
Jen., Jenyns.
K. & B., Keyserling and Blasius.
Lac., Lacépède.
Lath., Latham.
Latr., Latreille.
Laur., Laurenti.
L., Linnæus.
Less., Lesson.
Macg., Macgillivray.
Mœhr., Mœhring.
Mont., Montagu.
Müll., Müller.
M. & H., Müller and Henle.
Natt., Natterer.
Naum., Naumann.
Nilss., Nilsson.
Pall., Pallas.
Parn., Parnell.
Penn., Pennant.
Raf., Rafinesque.
Reich., Reichenbach.
Retz., Retzius.

Rich., Richardson.
Rond., Rondeletius.
Sav., Savigny.
Schreb., Schreber.
Scop., Scopoli.
Steph., Stephens.
Sw., Swainson.
Temm., Temminck.
Thoms., Thomson.

Val., Valenciennes.
Vieill., Vieillot.
Vig., Vigors.
Walb., Walbaum.
Wagl., Wagler.
Wagn., Wagner.
Will., Willughby.
Wils., Wilson.
Yarr., Yarrell.

The names in *italics* indicate those animals that are not regarded as truly indigenous; a name after a genus between inverted commas shows that the authority was anterior to 1766; = means that it is a synonym; *inc.* that such a group or genus is included in the one adopted; and *pt.* that the adopted group or genus is only a part of a larger group or genus. Only the more important synonyms are given, the English and the commonly known local names.

BRITISH VERTEBRATE ANIMALS.

Class 1. **PISCES.** (Fishes.)

ACRANIA.
= Pharyngobranchii and Leptocardii.

AMPHIOXIDÆ.
Amphioxus, *Yarr.*
= Branchiostoma, *Costa.*

A. lanceolatus (*Pall.*). Lancelet.
= Limax lanceolatus, *Pall.*

CYCLOSTOMI.
= Marsipobranchii.

PETROMYZONTIDÆ.
Myxine, *L.*
= Gastrobranchus, *Bl.*

M. glutinosa, *L.* Hag, Glutinous Hag, Borer.

Petromyzon, *L.*

P. marinus, *L.* Lamprey.
P. fluviatilis, *L.* River-Lamprey, Lampern.
P. Planeri, *Bl.* Planer's Lamprey.
 [Ammocœtes branchialis, *L.* Pride, Sand-Pride, Mud-Lamprey, the larval form.]

TELEOSTEI.
(*Physostomi.*)

MURÆNIDÆ.
Anguilla, *Cuv.*

A. vulgaris, *Turt.* Eel, Snig-Eel, Grig, Glut.
— acutirostris, *Yarr.*, var.
— latirostris, *Yarr.*, var.

Conger, *Cuv.*
C. vulgaris, *Cuv.* Conger, Conger-Eel.

Muræna, L.
M. helena, L.

[Leptocephalus is a larval form due to an arrest of development of probably "various forms of marine fishes," and perishing "without having attained the characters of the perfect animal" (*cf.* Günther, Intr. Fishes, p. 81).]

CLUPEIDÆ.
Clupea, *L.*
inc. Alosa, *Cuv.* (Alausa, *Val.*).

C. pilchardus, *Bl.* Pilchard. [The smaller Pilchards are known as Sardines.]
— Leachii, *Yarr.*, var.
C. harengus, *L.* Herring.
 [The Whitebait, *Clupea latulus*, Cuv. (*Rogenia alba*, Val.), the young.]
C. sprattus, *L.* Sprat, Garvie.
C. alosa, *L.* Shad.
C. finta, *Cuv.* Twaite Shad.

Engraulis, *Cuv.*
E. encrasicholus (*L.*). Anchovy.

CYPRINIDÆ.
Cobitis, *L.*
inc. Nemachilus, *Hasselt.*

C. barbatula, *L.*, "*Rond.*" Loach or Loche, Beardie.
C. tænia, *L.* Groundling.
= Tænia cornuta, *Will.*; Botia tænia, *Gray.*

Barbus, *Cuv.*
B. vulgaris, *Flem.* Barbel.

Alburnus, *Häckel.*
A. lucidus, *Häckel.* Bleak.
= Ausonii, *Gesn.*; Leuciscus alburnus, *Flem.*

Abramis, *Cuv.*
A. brama (*L.*). Bream, Carp-Bream.
= Cyprinus latus, *Aldr.*
A. blicca, *Bl.* White Bream.

Leuciscus, *Cuv.*
L. rutilus (*L.*). Roach.
= Rutilus Gesneri, *Aldr.*
L. vulgaris, *Flem.* Dace, Graining.
— Lancastriensis, *Yarr.*, var.
L. cephalus (*L.*). Chub.
L. idus (L.). Ide. [Orfe, a domestic var. having "the golden hue of semi-albinism."]
L. erythrophthalmus (*L.*). Rudd.
L. cæruleus, *Yarr.* Blue Roach.
L. phoxinus (*L.*). Minnow.
= Cyprinus aphya, *L.*

Gobio, *Cuv.*
G. fluviatilis, *Flem.* Gudgeon.

Tinca, *Cuv.*
T. vulgaris, *Flem.* Tench.
= aurata, *Cuv.*, var.

Cyprinus, *L.*
C. carpio, *L.* Carp. [Introduced in 1614.]

Carassius, *Nilss.*
C. vulgaris, *Nordmann.* Crucian Carp.
C. gibelio, *Bl.* Crouger, Prussian Carp.
C. auratus (*L.*). Goldfish. [Introduced in 1691.]

SCOMBRESOCIDÆ.

Scombresox, *Lac.*
S. saurus, *Flem.* Skipper, Saury Pike.

Belone, *Cuv.*
B. vulgaris, *Flem.* Garpike, Greenbone.
= Acus vulgaris, *Gesn.*

Exocœtus, L.
E. volitans, L. Flying-fish.
E. exiliens, Bl. Greater Flying-fish.
= *Mugil alatus*, Rond.

ESOCIDÆ.

Esox, *L.*
E. lucius, *L.* Pike, Jack, Pickerell, Gedd.

SALMONIDÆ.

Argentina, *L.*

A. sphyræna, *L.* Argentine. [Hebridal Smelt, the young.]

Thymallus, *Cuv.*

T. vulgaris, *Nilss.* Grayling.

Osmerus, *Cuv.*

O. eperlanus (*L.*). Smelt.

Coregonus, *Cuv.*

C. oxyrhynchus (L.).
C. clupeoides, *Lac.* Gwyniad, Powan.
    =? Salmo lavaretus, *L.*
C. vandesius, *Rich.* Vendace.
C. pollan, *Thoms.* Pollan.

Salmo, *L.*

S. salar, *L.* Salmon. [Parr or Pink, Smolt, and Grilse the earlier stages; Kelt after spawning.]
S. trutta, *L.* Salmon-Peel, Sea-Trout, White.
    = eriox, *Flem.*; = Trutta salmonata, *Ray.*
S. fario, *L.* Common Trout.
    = Trutta fluviatilis, *Ray.*
S. alpinus, *L.* Alpine Charr.
  — umbla, *L.*, var.; — salvelinus, *L.*, var.*
[*S. fontinalis*, Mitchell. Brook-Trout. Introduced.]

---

* In addition to the above, Dr. Günther enumerates the following "very insufficiently characterized" British "species":—

    S. Cambricus, *Don.* Sewen, Grey, Blue Poll.
    S. brachypoma, *Günth.*
    S. Gallivensis, *Günth.* Galway Sea-Trout.
    S. Orcadensis, *Günth.*
    S. ferox, *C. & V.* Great Lake Trout.
    S. stomachicus, *Günth.* Gillaroo Trout.

SCOPELIDÆ.

Paralepis, Cuv.
P. coregonoides, Risso.

STERNOPTYCHIDÆ.

Argyropelecus, Cocco.
A. hemigymnus, Cocco.

Maurolicus, Cocco.
M. Pennantii (Walb.). Argentine.
= Scopelus Humboldtii, Risso.

(*Anacanthini.*)

PLEURONECTIDÆ.

Hippoglossus, *Cuv.*
H. vulgaris, *Flem.* Halibut, Lady-Fluke.

Hippoglossoides, *Gottsche.*
H. limandoides (*Bl.*). Long Dab, Rough Dab, Sand-necker.

Rhombus, *Cuv.*
R. maximus (*L.*). Turbot. [Pleuronectes cyclops, *Don.*, probably a young Turbot.]
R. lævis, *Gottsche.* Brill, Pearl, Kite, Brett.

S. nigripinnis, *Günth.*
S. Levenensis, *Walker.* Loch-Leven Trout.
S. Killinensis, *Günth.* Loch-Killin Charr.
S. Willughbii, *Günth.* Windermere Charr.
S. Perisii, *Günth.* Torgoch.
S. Grayi, *Günth.* Freshwater Herring.
S. Colii, *Günth.* Enniskillen Charr.

Cf. Intr. Fish. pp. 664-666, and Cat. Fish. vi. pp. 34-138.

Zeugopterus, *Gottsche.*
= Phrynorhombus, *Günth.*

Z. unimaculatus (*Risso*). Eckström's Topknot.
= Rhombus punctatus, *Yarr.*

Z. punctatus (*Bl.*). Whiff, Browny, Müller's Topknot.
= Pleuronectes hirtus, *Müll.*

Arnoglossus, *Bleek.*

A. laterna (*Walb.*). Lantern-fish, Scald-fish, Megrim.
A. megastoma (*Don.*). Whiff, Carter, Sail-Fluke.
= Passer Cornubiensis, *Jago*; = Zeugopterus velivolans, *Rich.*

Pleuronectes, *L.*
inc. Platessa, *Cuv.*

P. platessa, *L.* Plaice.
P. microcephalus, *Don.* Smear-Dab, Lemon-Dab, Mary-Sole, French Sole.
P. cynoglossus, *L.* Pole, Long Flounder.
= Platessa pola, *Cuv.*; = elongata, *Yarr.*

P. limanda, *L.* Dab.
P. flesus, *L.* Flounder, Fluke, Butt.
= Passer fluviatilis, *Ray.*

Solea, *Günth.*
inc. Monochirus, *Yarr.*

S. vulgaris, *Quensel.* Sole.
S. lascaris, *Risso.* Lemon Sole.
= pegusa, *Yarr.*; = aurantiaca, *Günth.*

S. variegata (*Don.*). Banded Sole.
= Mangili, *Bon.*

S. lutea (*Risso*). Little Sole, Red Sole, Solenette.
= lingula, *Jenyns*; = minuta, *Günth.*

MACRURIDÆ.

Coryphænoides, Gunn.

C. rupestris, Gunn.
= *Macrurus Norvegicus*, Nilss.

OPHIDIIDÆ.

Ammodytes, L.

A. tobianus, *L.*   Launce, Lesser Sand-Eel.
A. lanceolatus, *Lesauvage.*   Greater Sand-Eel.
= lancea, *Cuv.*; = tobianus, *Yarr.*
A. cicerellus, Raf.
= *Siculus*, Swainson.

Fierasfer, Cuv.
= *Echiodon*, Thomson.

F. dentatus, Cuv.
= *Echiodon Drummondi*, Thomson.

Ophidium, L.

O. barbatum, L.
[O. imberbe, *L.*, the larval form of Anguilla vulgaris.]

GADIDÆ.

Molva, *Nilss.*

M. vulgaris, *Flem.*   Ling.
= Asellus longus, *Will.*

Lota, *Cuv.*

L. vulgaris, *Cuv.*   Burbot, Eel-Pout.

Motella, *Cuv.*

M. mustela (*L.*).   Sea-Loche, Five-bearded Rockling, Whistler.

M. cimbria (*L.*). Four-bearded Rockling.
M. tricirrata (*Bl.*). Three-bearded Rockling.
= maculata, *Günth.*; = Couchia argentata, *Günth.*
M. macrophthalma, Günth.
 [Ciliata glauca, *Couch* (Couchia minor, *Thomson*), the Mackerel-Midge, is the young of Motella mustela.]

Brosmius, *Cuv.*

B. brosme, *Müll.* Torsk or Tusk.

Raniceps, *Cuv.*

R. raninus (*L.*). Trifurcated Hake.

Phycis, *Bl.*

P. blennioides, *Bl.* Fork-Beard.

Merluccius, *Cuv.*

M. vulgaris, *Flem.* Hake.

Gadus, *L.*

inc. Morrhua, *Cuv.*, and Merlangus, *Cuv.*

G. morrhua, *L.* Cod.
G. æglefinus, *L.* Haddock.
 = Asellus major, *Aldr.*
G. luscus, *L.* Bib, Whiting-Pout.
G. minutus, *L.* Poor- or Power-Cod.
G. merlangus, *L.* Whiting.
G. albus, *Yarr.* Potassou.
G. virens, *L.* Coal-fish.
G. pollachius, *L.* Pollack.
 [G. callarias, *L.* Dorsch, the young of the Cod.]

(*Pharyngognathi.*)

LABRIDÆ.
Labrus, *L.*

L. maculatus, *L.* Ballan Wrasse, Old Wife.
  = bergylta, *Asc.*
— comber, *L.*, var.
  [L. lineatus, *Don.*, Green-fish; pusillus, *Jenyns*, Corkling (= Crenilabrus multidentatus, *Thomson*), the young.]
L. mixtus, *L.* Cook, Striped Wrasse, Cuckoo Wrasse.
  = coquus, *L.*; = trimaculatus, *Gm.*; = variegatus, *Gm.*
  [L. carneus, *Bl.* Red Wrasse, the female.]

Ctenolabrus, *Cuv.*

C. rupestris, *L.* Jago's Goldsinny.

Crenilabrus, *Cuv.*

C. melops (*L.*). Corkwing, Goldsinny, Connor, Gilthead, Golden Maid.
  = Labrus Cornubicus (*Gm.*); = Norvegicus (*Bl.*).

Acantholabrus, Cuv.

A. Palloni, Risso. Scale-rayed Wrasse.
  = *Couchii*, C. & V.

Centrolabrus, *Günth.*

C. exoletus (*L.*). Rock-Cook, Small-mouthed Wrasse.

Julis, Risso.
Coris, Lac., not L.

J. *Mediterranea*, Risso. Rainbow Wrasse.
  = *Coris julis*, Günth.

(*Acanthopterygii.*)

CENTRISCIDÆ.
Centriscus, L.
C. scolopax, L.   Trumpet-fish.

GOBIESOCIDÆ.
Lepadogaster, *Gouan.*
L. Gouani, *Risso.*   Cornish Sucker.
L. Candollei, *Risso.*   Connemara Sucker.
L. bimaculatus (*Penn.*).   Bimaculated Sucker.

CEPOLIDÆ.
Cepola, L.
C. rubescens, L.   Red Band-fish.

MUGILIDÆ.
Mugil, *L.*
M. capito, *Cuv.*   Grey Mullet.
M. chelo, *Cuv.*   Lesser Grey Mullet.
— curtus, *Cuv.*, var.
— septentrionalis, *Cuv.*, var.
— octoradiatus, *Günth.*, var.
[M. cephalus, *L.* Under this name Linnæus confounded two species; Cuvier has retained it for the Mediterranean form.]

ATHERINIDÆ.
Atherina, *L.*
A. presbyter, *Cuv.*   Sand-Smelt.
A. Boyeri, Risso.   Boyer's Atherine.

TRACHYPTERIDÆ.

Trachypterus, *Gouan.*
Bogmarus, *Bl.*

T. arcticus, *Brünn.*   Deal-fish, Vaagmaer.

Regalecus, Brünn.
= *Gymnetrus*, Bl.

R. Banksii, Cuv.   Oar-fish, Ribbon-fish, King of the Herrings.
= *G. Hawkinsii*, Bl.

BLENNIIDÆ.

Anarrhicas, *L.*
A. lupus, *L.*   Wolf-fish, Cat-fish, Sea-Wolf, Sea-Cat.

Blennius, *L.*
B. gattorugine, *Bl.*   Tompot.
B. galerita, *L.*   Montagu's Blenny.
= Montagui, *Flem.*
B. ocellaris, *Bl.*   Butterfly Blenny.
B. pholis, *L.*   Shanny, Bullcod.

Carelophus, *Kröyer.*
= Blenniops, *Nilss.*

C. Ascanii, *Walb.*   Yarrell's Blenny.
= Blennius palmicornis, *Yarr.*; = Yarrellii, *C. & V*

Centronotus, *Bl.*
C. gunnellus (*L.*).   Gunnel-fish, Butter-fish.
= Gunnellus Cornubiensium, *Will.*

Lumpenus, Reinh.
L. lampetræformis (Walb.).
= *Stichæus Islandicus*, Günth.

Zoarces, *Cuv.*

Z. viviparus, *L.* Viviparous Blenny, Eel-Pout, Guffer.

LOPHIIDÆ.

Lophius, *L.*

L. piscatorius, *L.* Angler, Frog-fish, Fishing-Frog, Sea-Devil, Wide-gab.

CYCLOPTERIDÆ.

Liparis, *Cuv.*

L. vulgaris, *Flem.* Sea-Snail, Unctuous Sucker.
L. Montagui, *Don.* Montagu's Sea-Snail.

Cyclopterus, *L.*

C. lumpus, *L.* Lump-fish, Cock-paddle, Sea-Owl.
    = Lumpus Anglorum, *Gesn.*

GOBIIDÆ.

Gobius, *L.*

G. Ruthensparii, *Euphr.* Two-spotted Goby.
    = bipunctatus, *Yarr.*
G. paganellus, *Gm.*
    = niger, *Yarr.*
G. niger, *L.* Black Goby, Rock-fish.
G. minutus, *Gm.* Spotted Goby, Yellow Goby.
    = gracilis, *Yarr.*; = ? unipunctatus, *Parn.*
G. gracilis, *Parn.* Little Goby, Spotted Goby, Polewig.
    = minutus, *Couch*; = attenuatus, *Couch*; = Parnelli, *Day.*
G. pictus, Malm.
G. quadrimaculatus, Cuv.
    = *Jeffreysii*, Günth.

Gobiosoma, *Günth.*
Crystallogobius, Gill.

G. Nilssoni, "*Düb. & Kor.*"

Aphia, *Risso.*
A. pellucida, *Nardo.*
= Latrunculus albus, *Günth.*

Callionymus, *L.*
C. lyra, *L.*   Gemmeous Dragonet, Yellow Skulpin, Gowdie.

[C. dracunculus, *L.*   Sordid Dragonet, Dusky Skulpin, female of *C. lyra.*]

C. *maculatus*, Bon.   Spotted Dragonet.

XIPHIIDÆ.

Xiphias, *L.*
X. gladius, *L.*   Sword-fish.

CARANGIDÆ.

Caranx, *Lac.*
inc. Trachurus, C. & V.

C. trachurus, *L.*   Scad, Horse-Mackerel.
= Trachurus trachurus, *Günth.*

Naucrates, Cuv.
= *Centronotus*, Lac., not Bl.

N. *ductor* (L.).   Pilot-fish.
= *Gasterosteus ductor*, L.

Pammelas, Günth.
P. *perciformis* (Mitch.).

Lichia, Cuv.

L. glauca (L.).
= *Scomber glaucus*, L.

Capros, Lac.

C. aper (*L.*). Boar-fish.
= Aper Rondeletii, *Will.*; Zeus aper, *L.*

SCOMBRIDÆ.

Scomber, L.

S. scombrus, *C. & V.* Mackerel.
— punctatus, *Couch*, var.
S. *pneumatophorus*, Laroche.
S. Colias, *Gm.* Spanish Mackerel.
= Colias Rondeletii, *Ray.*

Thynnus, Cuv.

T. vulgaris, C. & V. Tunny.
T. pelamys, Cuv. Bonito.

Orcynus, Cuv.

O. germo (Lac.). Albacore, Germon.
= *Scomber alalonga*, Gm.

Pelamys, C. & V.

P. Sarda (Bl.). Short-finned Tunny.

Auxis, C. & V.

A. Rochei (Risso). Plain Bonito.
= *vulgaris*, Yarr.

Echeneis, L.

E. remora, L. Sucking-fish, Remora.

CYTTIDÆ.

Zeus, *L.*

Z. faber, *L.*   Dory, John Dory.

CORYPHÆNIDÆ.

Lampris, *Retz.*

L. luna (*Gm.*).   Opah, Sun-fish.
= Zeus luna, *Gm.*

Schedophilus, Cocco.

S. medusophagus (Cocco).
= *Centrolophus medusophagus*, Cocco.

Luvarus, Raf.

L. imperialis, Raf.

Brama, *Risso*.

B. Raii (*Bl.*).   Ray's Sea-Bream.

STROMATEIDÆ.

Centrolophus, Lac.

C. *pompilus*, Cuv.   Black-fish.
C. *Britannicus*, Günth.

TRICHIURIDÆ.

Lepidopus, Gouan.

L. *caudatus*, Euphr.   Scabbard-fish.
= *argyreus*, Cuv.; = *Ziphotheca tetradens*, Mont.

Trichiurus, L.
T. *lepturus,* L.   Blade-fish, Hair-tail.

SCIÆNIDÆ.

Sciæna, *Cuv.*
S. aquila, *Risso.*   Stone-Basse, Maigre.

TRACHINIDÆ.

Trachinus, *L.*
T. draco, *L.*   Greater Weever, Sting-fish.
= Draco marinus, *Rond.*
T. vipera, *Cuv.*   Lesser Weever, Otterpike.

TRIGLIDÆ.

Trigla, *L.*
T. cuculus, *L.*   Red Gurnard, Rock-Mullet.
= pini, *Bl.*
T. lineata, *L.*   Streaked Gurnard.
T. hirundo, *L.*   Tub, Sapphirine Gurnard.
T. lyra, *L.*   Piper.
T. gurnardus, *L.*   Grey Gurnard.
T. lucerna, *Brünn.*   Long-finned Captain.

Peristethus, Kaup.
= *Peristedion,* Lac.
P. *cataphractus* (L.).   Mailed Gurnard.

Agonus, *Bl.*
= Aspidophorus, *Lac.*
A. cataphractus (*L.*).   Pogge, Bullhead.

Cottus, *L.*

C. scorpius, *Bl.*   Sea-Scorpion, Poison-pate.
C. bubalis, *Euphr.*   Father-lasher, Sting-fish.
C. gobio, *L.*   Miller's Thumb.
C. quadricornis, *Bl.*

SCORPÆNIDÆ.

Sebastes, *Cuv.*

S. Norvegicus, *Cuv.*   Bergylt, Norway Haddock.

SPARIDÆ.

Pagrus, C. & V.

P. vulgaris, C. & V.
— *orphus,* Yarr., var.

Chrysophrys, Cuv.

C. aurata (L.).   Gilthead.

Pagellus, *Cuv.*

P. centrodontus, *C. & V.*   Bream, Sea-Bream, Red Bream. (Chad the young.)
P. bogaraveo (*Brünn.*).   Spanish Bream.
P. Owenii, *Günth.*   ? Red Gilthead.
P. acarne (Risso).   Axillary Bream.
P. erythrinus (*L.*).   Braize, Becker, King of the Bream.
    = Pagrus vulgaris, *Yarr.*

Box, *Cuv.*

B. boops (L.).   Bogue.
    = *vulgaris,* Cuv.

Cantharus, *Cuv.*

C. lineatus (*Mont.*).   Old Wife, Black Bream.
= griseus, *Yarr.*

MULLIDÆ.
Mullus, *L.*

M. barbatus, *L.*   Red Mullet.
  [M. surmuletus, *L.*, var. ?, probably the female according to Dr. Günther.]

PERCIDÆ.
Perca, *L.*

P. fluviatilis, *L.*, "*Rond.*"   Perch.

Labrax, *Cuv.*

L. lupus, *Cuv.*   Basse.

Acerina, *Cuv.*

A. cernua (*L.*).   Ruffe, Pope.
= Cernua fluviatilis, *Gesn.*

Serranus, *Cuv.*

S. cabrilla (*L.*).   Sea-Perch, Comber.
S. gigas (Brünn.).   Dusky Perch.

[*Huro*, C. & V.
H. nigricans, C. & V.   Black Basse.   Introduced.]

Denter, Cuv.
D. vulgaris, Cuv.   Toothed Gilthead.

Polyprion, Cuv.
P. cernium, Cuv.   Stone-Basse.

GASTROSTEIDÆ.

Gastrosteus, *L.*
ino. Spinachia, *Flem.*

G. aculeatus, *L.* Stickleback, Three-spined Stickleback.
= Pungitius Alberti, *Forst.*
— trachurus, *Cuv.*, var.
— leiurus, *Cuv.*, var.
— semiarmatus, *Cuv.*, var.
— brachycentrus, *Cuv.*, var.
G. spinulosus, *Jen. & Yarr.* Four-spined Stickleback.
G. pungitius, *L.* Nine-spined Stickleback.
G. spinachia, *L.* Fifteen-spined Stickleback, Sea-Adder.

LOPHOBRANCHII.

SYNGNATHIDÆ.

Syngnathus, *L.*
S. acus, *L.* Greater Pipe-fish.

Nerophis, *Raf.*
N. æquoreus (*L.*). Ocean Pipe-fish.
N. ophidion (*L.*). Snake Pipe-fish.
N. lumbriciformis (*Yarr.*). Little Pipe-fish.

Siphonostoma, *Kaup.*
S. typhle (*L.*). Broad-nosed Pipe-fish.

HIPPOCAMPIDÆ.

Hippocampus, *Leach.*
H. antiquorum, *Leach.* Sea-Horse.

PLECTOGNATHI.
inc. Sclerodermi and Gymnodontes.

OSTRACIONTIDÆ.
Ostracion, L.
O. quadricornis, L.   Four-horned Trunk-fish.

BALISTIDÆ.
Balistes, L.
B. maculatus, Gm.   File-fish.
B. capriscus, Gm.

ORTHAGORISCIDÆ.
Tetrodon, L.
T. lagocephalus, L.   Pennant's Globe-fish.
   = *stellatus,* Don.

Orthagoriscus, *Bl.*
O. mola, *Bl.*   Short Sun-fish, Molebut.
O. truncatus, *Flem.*   Oblong Sun-fish.

CHONDROPTERYGII.
= Elasmobranchii; Palæichthyes, *pt.*

Batoidei.   (RAYS.)

RAIIDÆ.
Raia, *L.*
inc. Dasybatis, *Bon.*
R. batis, *L.*   Skate.

R. macrorhynchus, *Raf.* Flapper Skate.
   = intermedia, *Parn.*; = rostrata, *Bl.*

R. marginata, *Lac.* Burton Skate.
   = alba, *Lac.*; = oxyrhynchus, *Mont.*

R. oxyrhynchus, *L.* Long-nosed Skate.
   = mucronata, *Yarr.*; = rostrata, *Risso*; = vomer, *Fr.*

R. fullonica, *L.*, "*Rond.*" Shagreen Ray.
   = chagrinea, *Penn.*; = aspera, *Flem.*

R. clavata, *L.*, "*Rond.*" Thornback.
   = rubus, *Bl.*

R. maculata, *Mont.* Homelyn Ray.
   = miraletus, *Yarr.*

R. microcellata, *Mont.* Painted Ray, Small-eyed Ray.

R. radiata, *Don.* Starry Ray.

R. circularis, *Couch.* Sandy Ray, Cuckoo-Ray.
   = radula, *Yarr.*

TRYGONIDÆ.

Trygon, *M. & H.*

T. pastinaca (*L.*). Sting-Ray.
   = Pastinaca marina, *Gem.*

MYLIOBATIDÆ.

Myliobatis, Cuv.

M. aquila, Cuv. Eagle-Ray, Whip-Ray.
   = *Aquila marina*, Rond.

Cephaloptera, Dum.
   = Dicerobatis, *Blain.*

C. Giornæ, Lac. Ox-Ray, Sea-Devil.
   = *Squalus edentulus*, Giorna.

TORPEDINIDÆ.
Torpedo, Dum.
T. *nobiliana*, Bon. Cramp-Ray, Numb-fish.
= *hebetans*, Lowe; = *Walshii*, Thoms.

T. *marmorata*, Risso.
= *vulgaris*, Flem.

Selachoidei. (SHARKS.)
SQUATINIDÆ.
Squatina, *Dum.*
= Rhina, *Klein*, not *Latr.*

S. vulgaris, *Flem.* Monk-fish, Angel-fish.
= Rhina squatina, *Raf.*

SPINACIDÆ.
Echinorhinus, *Blain.*
E. spinosus (*Gm.*). Spinous Shark.
= Scymnus spinosus, *Cuv.*

Læmargus, Müll.
= *Dalatias*, Raf.

L. *borealis* (Scoresby). Greenland Shark.
= *microcephalus*, Kröyer.

Acanthias, *Risso.*
A. vulgaris, *Risso.* Dog-fish, Picked Dog-fish, Bone-Dog.
= Spinax acanthias, *Cuv.*

Centrina, Cuv.
C. *Salviani* (Risso).
= *Galeus centrinus*, Gesn.

SCYLLIIDÆ.

Scyllium, *Cuv.*

S. canicula (*Bl.*). Small-spotted Dog-fish, Nursehound, Morgay.
    = Canicula Aristotelis, *Gesn.*
S. catulus (*L.*). Large-spotted Dog-fish, Bounce.

Pristiurus, Bon.
P. *melanostoma*, Bon. Black-mouthed Dog-fish.

NOTIDANIDÆ.

Notidanus, Cuv.
N. *griseus* (Gm.). Brown Shark.

LAMNIDÆ.

Lamna, *Cuv.*
L. Cornubica, *Schn.* Porbeagle, Beaumaris Shark.
    = Canis carcharias, *Aldr.*

Alopecias, *M. & H.*
A. vulpes, *Cuv.* Thresher, Sea-Fox, Fox-Shark, Sea-Ape.

Selache, *Cuv.*
S. maxima (*L.*). Basking Shark, Sun-fish.

CARCHARIIDÆ.

Carcharias, *Cuv.*
C. vulgaris, *Cuv.* White Shark.
    = Squalus carcharias, *L.*, "*Gunn.*
C. glaucus (*L.*). Blue Shark.

Mustelus, *Cuv.*

M. vulgaris, *M. & H.*   Smooth Hound.
= lævis, *Auct. Br.*

Zygæna, *Cuv.*
= *Sphyrna*, Raf.

Z. malleus, *Cuv.*   Hammer-headed Shark.
= Sphyrna zygæna, *Raf.*

Galeus, *Cuv.*

G. vulgaris, *Cuv.*   Tope, Miller's Dog, Penny Dog.
= Canis galeus, *Will.*

HOLOCEPHALI.
Palæichthyes, *pt.*

CHIMÆRIDÆ.

Chimæra, *L.*

C. monstrosa, *L.*   Rabbit-fish, King of the Herrings.
= Simia marina, *Gesn.*

GANOIDEI.
Palæichthyes, *pt.*

ACIPENSERIDÆ.

Acipenser, *L.*

A. sturio, *L.*   Sturgeon.

Class 2. **AMPHIBIA.**

URODELA.

SALAMANDRIDÆ.

Molge, *Merrem.*
= Triton, *Laur.*, not *L.*; *inc.* Lissotriton, *Bell.*

M. cristata (*Laur.*). Newt, Eft.
= Triton Bibronii, *Bell*, var.

M. punctata (*Daud.*). Smooth Newt.

M. palmipes (*Latr.*).
= Triton vittatus, *Gray.*

BATRACHIA.

RANIDÆ.

Rana, *L.*

R. temporaria, *L.* Frog.
— Scotica, *Bell*, var.
[*R. esculenta*, L. Edible Frog.
— *Lessonæ*, Camerano, var. Introduced.]
— typica, *Boulenger*, var.

BUFONIDÆ.

Bufo.

B. vulgaris, *Laur.* Toad.
B. calamita, *Laur.* Natterjack.

Class 3. **REPTILIA.**

OPHIDIA.

COLUBRIDÆ.

Coluber, *L.*
= Pelias, *Merrem*; Vipera, *Schleg.*, not *Gray*.

C. berus, *L.* Viper, Adder.
= prester, *L.* Black Viper, var.

Coronella, *Laur.*
C. Austriaca, *Laur.*

Natrix, *Laur.*
= Tropidonotus, *Kuhl.*

N. torquata (*Lac.*), "*Ray.*" Snake.
= Coluber natrix, *L.*

SAURIA.
= Lacertilia.

LACERTIDÆ.

Lacerta, *L.*
L. agilis, *L.* Sand-Lizard.
= stirpium, *Daud.*
[*L. viridis*, Daud. Occurs in Jersey.]

Zootoca, *Wagl.*

Z. vivipara (*Jacq.*). Common Lizard.
=Lacerta agilis, *Flem.*

ANGUIDÆ.

Anguis, *L.*

A. fragilis, *L.* Blind-worm, Slow-worm.

CHELONIA.
= *Testudinata.*

TESTUDINIDÆ.

Testudo, L.

[*T. Europæa,* L. Tortoise. Introduced.]

CHELONIIDÆ.

Chelonia, Brong.

C. imbricata (L.). Hawk's-bill Turtle.

Sphargis, Gray.
= *Coriudo,* Flem.

S. coriacea (L.). Leathery Turtle.

Class 4. **AVES.** (Birds.)

PICI.

(Scansores, *pt.*; Zygodactyli, *pt.*; Picariæ, *pt.*; Volucres, *pt.*)

= Coleomorphæ.

PICIDÆ.

Gecinus, *Boie.*

G. viridis (*L.*). Green Woodpecker, Rain-fowl.
= Picus viridis, *Gesn.*

Picus, *L.*
= Dendrocopus, *Koch.*

P. major, *L.* Greater Spotted Woodpecker.
= discolor, *Fisch.*

P. minor, *L.* Lesser Spotted Woodpecker.
P. medius, L. Middle Spotted Woodpecker.
P. villosus, Forst. Hairy Woodpecker.
P. pubescens, L. Downy Woodpecker.

Dryocopus, Boie.

D. martius (L.). Great Black Woodpecker.
= Picus maximus, Aldr.

Colaptes, Sw.

C. auratus (L.). Golden-winged Woodpecker.
= Cuculus auratus, L. (Syst. Nat. ed. 10).

Apternus, Sw.
Picoides, Lac.

A. tridactylus (L.). Three-toed Woodpecker.

JYNGIDÆ.
Jynx, *L.*
Yunx, *Auct.*; Torquilla, *Briss.*

J. torquilla, *L.* Wryneck.

VOLITORES.
(Insessores, *pt.*; Fissirostres, *pt.*; Syndactyli, *pt.*; Oscines, *pt.*;
Volucres, *pt.*; Cypselomorphæ, *pt.*; Coccygomorphæ, *pt.*;
inc. Macrochires.)

CORACIIDÆ.
Coracias, L.
C. *garrula*, L. Roller.
= *Cornix cærulea*, Gesn.

UPUPIDÆ.
Upupa, *L.*
U. epops, *L.* Hoopoe.

MEROPIDÆ.
Merops, L.
M. *apiaster*, L. Bee-eater.
M. *Philippinus*, L. Blue-tailed Bee-eater.

ALCEDINIDÆ.
Alcedo, *L.*
inc. Ceryle, *Boie.*

A. ispida, *L.* Kingfisher.
A. *alcyon*, L. Belted Kingfisher.

CAPRIMULGIDÆ.
Caprimulgus, *L.*

C. Europæus, *L.*   Goatsucker, Nightjar, Dor-Hawk, Fern-Owl.
C. ruficollis, Temm.   Red-necked Goatsucker.

HIRUNDINIDÆ.
Cotile, *Boie.*

C. riparia (*L.*).   Sand-Martin.

Chelidon, *Boie.*

C. urbica (*L.*).   House-Martin.

Hirundo, *L.*
inc. Tachycineta, *Cab.*

H. rustica, *L.*   Swallow.
  = domestica, *Gesn.*
H. rufula, Temm.   Red-rumped Swallow.
H. bicolor, Vieill.   White-bellied Swallow.
H. Savignyi, Steph.   Chestnut-bellied Swallow.

Progne, Boie.

P. purpurea (L.).   Purple Swallow.

CYPSELIDÆ.
Cypselus, *Ill.*

C. apus (*L.*).   Swift, Black Martin.
  = Hirundo apus, *L.*
C. alpinus (Scop.).   Alpine Swift.
  = Hirundo melba, *L.*

Acanthyllis, Boie.
= *Chætura*, Steph.

A. caudacuta (Lath.).

COCCYGES.
(Scansores, *pt.*; Zygodactyli, *pt.*; Picariæ, *pt.*; Volucres, *pt.*)
= Coccygomorphæ.

CUCULIDÆ.
Cuculus, *L.*
C. canorus, *L.* Cuckoo, Gowk.

Coccyzus, Vieill.

C. Americanus (L.). Yellow-billed Cuckoo.
C. erythrophthalmus (Wils.). Black-billed Cuckoo.

Coccystes, Gloger.
= *Oxylophus*, Sw.

C. glandarius (L.). Great Spotted Cuckoo.

PASSERES.
(Insessores, *pt.*; Oscines, *pt.*; Coracomorphæ, *pt.*; Ægithognathæ, *pt.*; *inc.* Tenuirostres, Dentirostres, Conirostres, and Magnirostres.)

CERTHIIDÆ.
Certhia, *L.*
C. familiaris, *L.* Creeper.

Tichodroma, Ill.

T. muraria (L.). Wall-creeper.

Sitta, *L.*
S. cæsia, *Wolf.* Nuthatch. [The South-western form of the Northern *S. Europæa*, L.]

LANIIDÆ.
Lanius, *L.*
inc. Enneoctonus, *Bois.*

L. excubitor, *L.* Butcher-bird, Shrike.
L. *major*, Pall. Pallas's Butcher-bird.
  [*L. excubitorides* (*L. Ludovicianus*, L.), mistaken for *L. major*.]
L. collurio, *L.* Red-backed Shrike, Flusher, Nine-killer.
L. *rutilus*, Lath. Woodchat.
  = *Pomeranus*, Sparrman; = *rufus*, Temm.; *auriculatus*, Müll.

Vireo, Vieill.
  = *Vireosylvia*, Bon.

V. *violaceus* (L.). Red-eyed Flycatcher.

MUSCICAPIDÆ.
Muscicapa, *L.*
inc. Butalis, *Bois*, and Erythrosterna, *Bon.*

M. atricapilla, *L.* Pied Flycatcher.
M. grisola, *L.* Spotted Flycatcher.
M. *parva*, Bechst. Red-breasted Flycatcher.

SYLVIIDÆ.
Sylvia, *Scop.*
inc. Curruca, *Briss.*

S. cinerea, *Bechst.* Whitethroat.
  = *rufa*, *Newton.*
S. curruca (*L.*). Lesser Whitethroat.
  = Curruca sylviella (*Yarr.*).
S. *orphea*, Temm. Orphean Warbler.

S. atricapilla (*L.*). Blackcap.
S. hortensis (*Gm.*). Garden-Warbler.
    = salicaria, *Newton.*
S. nisoria (Bechst.). Barred Warbler.

Hypolais, Brehm.
H. icterina (Vieill.). Icterine Warbler.

Phylloscopus, *Boie.*
inc. Phyllopneuste, *Meyer*, and Ficedula, *Koch.*

P. superciliosus (Gm.). Dalmatian Regulus.
    = *Regulus modestus*, Naum.
P. rufus (*Bechst.*). Chiffchaff, Lesser Pettychaps.
P. trochilus (*L.*). Willow-Wren.
P. sibilatrix (*Bechst.*). Wood-Wren.

Acrocephalus, *Naum.*
inc. Calamodyta, *Wolf*; Salicaria, *Selby*; Calamodus, *Kaup*; Dcustella, *Kaup*; Potamodus, *Kaup*; Calamoherpe, *Boie*; Sibilatrix, *Mucg.*; Cettia, *Bon.*; and Bradypterus, *Dresser.*

A. turdoides, Meyer. Great Reed-Warbler.
    = *arundinaceus* (L.).
A. streperus (*Vieill.*). Reed-Warbler.
    = Sylvia arundinacea, *Naum.*
A. palustris (*Bechst.*). Marsh-Warbler.
    = salicaria (*L.*).
A. aquaticus (Gm.).
A. phragmitis (*Bechst.*). Sedge-Warbler.
A. locustella (*Lath.*). Grasshopper-Warbler.
    = Locustella avicula, *Ray.*
A. luscinioides (Savi). Savi's Warbler.
A. sericea (Temm.). Cetti's Warbler.

Aëdon, Boie.
A. *galactodes* (Temm.). Rufous Warbler.

Melizophilus, *Leach*.
M. undatus (*Bodd.*). Dartford Warbler.
= Motacilla provincialis (*Gm.*).

Regulus, *Cuv.*
R. cristatus, *Koch*, "*Will.*" Golden-crested Wren.
R. *ignicapillus*, Temm. Fire-crested Wren.
R. *calendula* (L.). Ruby-crowned Wren.

Luscinia, *Brehm*.
= Daulias, *Boie*, and Philomela, *Selby*.
L. philomela (*Bon.*). Nightingale.
= Erithacus luscinia, *Seebohm*.

Erithacus, *Cuv.*
= Rubecula, *Brehm*.
E. rubecula (*L.*). Robin, Redbreast.

Ruticilla, *Brehm*.
R. phœnicura (*L.*). Redstart.
R. *tithys* (Scop.). Black Redstart.

Cyanecula, Brehm.
C. *Suecica* (L.). Bluethroat.
[C. *Wolfii* (Brehm), var.]

Pratincola, *Koch*.
Fruticicola, *MacG.*
P. rubetra (*L.*). Whinchat.
P. rubicola (*L.*). Stonechat.

Saxicola, *Bechst.*

S. œnanthe (*L.*). Wheatear.
S. stapazina, Vieill. Black-throated Wheatear.
S. deserti, Temm. Desert-Wheatear.

Accentor, *Bechst.*

A. modularis (*L.*). Hedge-Sparrow.
A. collaris (Scop.). Alpine Accentor.
 = *Sturnus collaris*, Soop.; = *Motacilla alpina*, Gm.

TURDIDÆ.

Turdus, *L.*

T. viscivorus, *L.* Missel-Thrush.
T. musicus, *L.* Thrush, Throstle, Greybird, Mavis.
T. iliacus, *L.*, " *Will.*" Redwing, Winnard.
T. pilaris, *L.*, " *Gesn.*" Fieldfare.
T. migratorius, L. American Robin.
T. varius, Pall. White's Thrush.
T. atrigularis, Temm. Black-throated Thrush.
T. torquatus, *L.* Ring-Ouzel.
T. Sibiricus, Pall. Siberian Thrush.
T. merula, *L.* Blackbird.

Petrocincla, Vig.
inc. Monticola, *Boie*, and Petrocossyphus, *Boie*.

P. *saxatilis* (Gm.). Rock-Thrush.
[P. *cyanus* (L.). Blue Thrush. Erroneously recorded.]

Pycnonotus, Kuhl.
= *Hæmatornis*, Sw.

P. *capensis* (L.). Gold-vented Thrush.
 = *Turdus aurigaster*, Yarr.
P. *barbatus* (Desf.). Dusky Bulbul.

CINCLIDÆ.

Cinclus, *Bechst.*

C. aquaticus, *Bechst.* Dipper, Water-Ouzel.
= Sturnus cinclus, *L.*
— *melanogaster*, Brehm. Black-bellied Dipper, var.

MOTACILLIDÆ.

Motacilla, *L.*
inc. Budytes, *Cuv.*

M. lugubris, *Temm.* Pied Wagtail, Dishwasher.
= Yarrelli, *Naum.*
M. alba, *L.* White Wagtail.
M. melanope, *Pall.* Grey Wagtail.
= boarula, *Temm.*; sulphurea, *Bechst.*
M. flava, *L.* Blue-headed Wagtail.
= neglecta, *Yarr.*
[M. *viridis*, Gm. Grey-headed Wagtail.
= *cinereocapilla*, Savi. Erroneously identified.]
M. campestris, *Pall.* Yellow Wagtail, Ray's Wagtail.
= Rayi, *Bon.*

Anthus, *Bechst.*
Alauda, *L., pt.*

A. trivialis (*L.*). Tree-Pipit, Titlark.
= arboreus, *Bechst.*
A. pratensis (*L.*). Meadow-Pipit.
A. obscurus (*Lath.*). Rock-Pipit.
A. spipoletta (*L.*). Water-Pipit.
A. *Ludovicianus* (Gm.). American Pipit.
A. campestris (*L.*). Tawny Pipit.
A. *Richardi*, Vieill. Richard's Pipit.
A. *cervinus* (Pall.). Red-throated Pipit.

TROGLODYTIDÆ.

Troglodytes, *Vieill.*
= Anorthura, *Rennie.*

T. parvulus, *Koch.* Wren.
= Passer troglodytes, *Gesn.*
— Hirtensis, *Seebohm*, var.

PARIDÆ.
Parus, *L.*
inc. Pœcile, *Kaup*, and Lophophanes, *Kaup.*

P. major, *L.* Great Titmouse.
P. cæruleus, *L.* Tomtit, Blue Titmouse.
P. ater, *L.* Cole-Tit, Cole-Mouse.
 [P. Britannicus, *Dresser* and *Sharpe*, the British form.]
P. palustris, *L.* Marsh-Tit.
P. cristatus, *L.*, "*Aldr.*" Crested Tit.

Acredula, *Kaup.*
= Mecistura, *Leach*; Orites, *Mahr.*

A. caudata (*L.*). Long-tailed Tit, Bottle-Tom.
 [A. rosea, *Blyth*, the ordinary British form.]

Panurus, *Koch.*
= Calamophilus, *Leach.*

P. biarmicus (*L.*). Bearded Tit.
= Lanius biarmicus, *L.* (Fn. Suec.).

FRINGILLIDÆ.
Loxia, *L.*

L. pityopsittacus, Bechst. Parrot Crossbill.
L. curvirostra, *L.* Crossbill.
L. leucoptera, Gm. White-winged Crossbill.
L. bifasciata (Brehm). Two-barred Crossbill.

Pyrrhula, *Briss.*
inc. Carpodacus, *Kaup.*

P. Europæa, *Vieill.* Bullfinch.
= vulgaris, *Yarr.*
P. *erythrina*, Pall. Scarlet Grosbeak.

Corythus, Cuv.
inc. Pinicola, Vieill., and *Strobilophaga*, Vieill.

C. *enucleator* (L.). Pine-Grosbeak.

Coccothraustes, *Cuv.*
C. vulgaris (*Pall.*). Hawfinch.

Ligurinus, *Koch.*
= Coccothraustes, *Auct. Br.*

C. chloris (*L.*). Greenfinch.

Passer, *Briss.*
= Pyrgita, *Cuv.*

P. domesticus (*L.*), "*Will.*" Sparrow.
P. montanus (*L.*), "*Aldr.*" Tree-Sparrow.

Fringilla, *L.*
F. cælebs, *L.* Chaffinch, Copper-Finch.
F. montifringilla, *L.* Brambling.

Carduelis, *Steph.*
inc. Chrysomitris, *Bois.*

C. elegans, *Steph.* Goldfinch.
C. spinus (*L.*). Siskin, Aberdevine.
C. *citrinella* (L.). Citril Finch.

Crithagra, Sw.
C. *chrysopyga*, Sw. Yellow-rumped Seed-eater.

Serinus, Koch.

S. *hortulanus*, Koch. Serin.
[*S. canarius* (L.). Canary. Introduced.]

Linota, Bon.
<small>inc. Ægiothus, *Cab.*</small>

L. cannabina (*L.*). Linnet, Greater Redpoll.
L. rufescens (*Vieill.*). Lesser Redpoll.
L. linaria (*L.*). Mealy Redpoll.
<small>= canescens, *Yarr.*; Linaria rubra, *Gesn.*</small>
L. Hornemanni, Holböll. Greenland Redpoll.
L. flavirostris (*L.*). Twite.
<small>= montium, *Yarr.*</small>

Spiza, Bon.

S. *ciris* (L.). Painted Bunting.

Emberiza, *L.*
<small>inc. Euspiza, *Bon.*; Crithophaga, *Gld.*; Glycyspina, *Cab.* and Schœnicola, *Bon.*</small>

E. miliaria, *L.* Bunting, Bunting-Lark.
<small>= alba, *Gesn.*</small>
E. citrinella, *L.* Yellow-Hammer.
E. cirlus, *L.* Cirl Bunting.
E. hortulanus, L. Ortolan.
E. rustica, Pall. Rustic Bunting.
E. pusilla, Pall. Little Bunting.
E. schœniclus, L. Reed-Bunting.
E. melanocephala, Scop. Black-headed Bunting.

Plectrophanes, *Meyer.*
<small>inc. Calcarius, *Bechst.*; and Centrophanes, *Kaup.*</small>

P. nivalis, *L.* Snow-Bunting.
P. *Lapponicus*, L. Lapland Bunting.

Zonotrichia, Sw.
Z. *albicollis* (Gm.).   White-throated Sparrow.

ALAUDIDÆ.
Alauda, *L.*
inc. Galerita, *Boie,* and Calandrella, *Kaup.*

A. arvensis, *L.*   Sky-Lark, Laverock.
A. arborea, *L.,* "*Will.*"   Wood-Lark.
A. cristata, *L.*   Crested Lark.
A. *brachydactyla,* Temm.   Short-toed Lark.

Otocorys, Bon.
O. *alpestris* (L.).   Shore-Lark.

Melanocorypha, Boie.
M. *calandra* (L.).   Calandra Lark.
M. *Sibirica* (Gm.).   White-winged Lark.

AMPELIDÆ.
Ampelis, L.
= *Bombycilla,* Vieill.

A. *garrula,* L.   Waxwing.
A. *cedrorum* (Vieill.).   Cedar-bird, American Waxwing.

ORIOLIDÆ.
Oriolus, L.
O. *galbula,* L.   Golden Oriole.
= *Coracias oriolus,* L. (Fn. Suec.).

STURNIDÆ.
Sturnus, *L.*
S. vulgaris, *L.*   Starling, Stare.

Sturnella, Vieill.

S. *magna* (L.).   Meadow-Lark.
= *Sturnus Ludovicianus,* Briss.

Scolecophagus, Sw.

S. *ferrugineus* (Gm.).   Rusty Grackle.

Agelæus, Vieill.

A. *phœniceus* (L.).   Red-winged Starling.

Pastor, Temm.
= *Thremmaphilus,* Macg.

P. *roseus* (L.).   Rose-coloured Starling.
= *Merula rosea,* Aldr.

Gracula, L.

G. *religiosa,* L.   Mino.

CORVIDÆ.

Corvus, *L.*

C. corax, *L.*   Raven.
C. corone, *L.*   Crow, Carrion-Crow.
C. cornix, *L.*   Hooded Crow.
C. frugilegus, *L.*   Rook.
C. monedula, *L.*   Jackdaw.

Pica, *Cuv.*

P. rustica, *Scop.*   Magpie.
= varia, *Gesn.*; caudata, *Flem.*

Garrulus, *Cuv.*

G. glandarius (*L.*).   Jay.
= Pica glandaria, *Gesn.*

Nucifraga, Briss.
= *Caryocatactes,* Cuv., "Gesn.
N. caryocatactes (L.). Nutcracker.

Fregilus, *Cuv.*
= Pyrrhocorax, *Vieill.*
F. graculus (*L.*). Chough, Cornish Chough.
= Graculus graculus, *Sharpe.*

COLUMBÆ.
= Gemitores and Peristeromorphæ; Volucres, *pt.*

COLUMBIDÆ.
Columba, *L.*
inc. Palumbus, *Gld.*
C. palumbus, *L.* Ring-Dove, Wood-Pigeon, Cushat.
C. œnas, *L.* Stock-Dove.
C. livia, *Bonn.* Rock-Dove.

Turtur, *Selby.*
T. auritus, *Gray.* Turtle-Dove.

Ectopistes, Sw.
E. migratorius (L.). Passenger Pigeon.

GALLINÆ.
= Rasores, Clamatores, and Alectoromorphæ.

PTEROCLIDÆ.
Syrrhaptes, Ill.
S. paradoxus (Pall.). Sand-Grouse.

TETRAONIDÆ.

Perdix, *Briss.*
inc. Starna, *Bon.,* and Caccabis, *Kaup;* Tetrao, *L., pt.*

P. cinerea, *Lath.* Partridge.
P. *rufa* (L.). Red-legged Partridge. [Introduced 1770.]
P. *petrosa* (Gm.). Barbary Partridge.

Ortyx, Steph.
O. *virginianus* (L.). Virginian Quail. [Introduced.]

Coturnix, *Bonn.*
C. communis, *Bonn.* Quail.
= dactylisonans, *Temm.*

Tetrao, *L.*
T. urogallus, *L.* Capercaillie, Wood-Grouse.
T. tetrix, *L.* Black Grouse.

Lagopus, *Briss.*
L. Scoticus (*Lath.*). Red Grouse.
L. mutus, *Leach.* Ptarmigan.
L. *rupestris* (Gm.). Rock-Ptarmigan.

Turnix, Bonn.
= *Hemipodius*, Temm.

T. *sylvatica* (Desf.). Andalusian Quail.
= *Hemipodius tachydromus*, Temm.

PHASIANIDÆ.

Phasianus, *L.*
P. Colchicus, *L.* Pheasant. [Naturalized.]

GRALLÆ.

= Grallatores.

(*Alectorides.*)

Cultrirostres, *pt.*; Geranomorphæ, *pt.*

OTIDIDÆ.

inc. Eupodotis, *Less.*; = Houbara, *Bon.*

Otis, *L.*

O. *tarda*, *L.*   Great Bustard.   [*Qu.* Extinct?]
O. *tetrax*, L.   Little Bustard.
= *Anas campestris*, Gesn.
O. *houbara*, Gm.   Ruffed Bustard.
= *Otis Macqueenii*, Gray.

GRUIDÆ.

Grus, Bechst.
= *Megalornis*, G. R. G.

G. *cinerea*, Bechst.   Crane.
= *Ardea grus*, L.

Anthropoides, Vieill.

A. *virgo* (L.).   Demoiselle.

Balearica, Briss.

B. *pavonina* (L.).   Balearic Crane.

PSOPHIIDÆ.

Psophia, L.

P. *crepitans*, L.   Trumpeter.

(Fulicariæ.)
= Macrodactyli; Geranomorphæ, *pt.*

RALLIDÆ.
Crex, *Bechst.*
= Ortygometra, *Steph.*, "*Ray.*"

C. *pratensis, Bechst.* Crake, Corn-Crake, Land-Rail.
= Ortygometra crex, *G. R. G.*

Porzana, *Vieill.*
inc. Zapornia, *Steph.*

P. *maruetta (Leach).* Spotted Crake.
= minor, *Aldr.*; Rallus porzana, *L.*

P. *Carolina* (L.). Carolina Rail.

P. *Baillonii* (Vieill.). Baillon's Crake.
= *Rallus Foljambei*, Mont.

P. *pusilla* (Mont.). Little Gallinule.
= *Rallus parvus*, Scop.

Rallus, *L.*
R. aquaticus, *L.*, "*Aldr.*" Rail, Water-Rail.

Gallinula, *Briss.*
G. chloropus (*L.*). Water-Hen, Moor-Hen.

Fulica, *L.*
F. atra, *L.* Coot.

Porphyrio, Briss.
P. *cæruleus*, Vandelli. Purple Gallinule.
= *Fulica porphyrio*, L.

P. *smaragnotus*, Temm. Green-backed Gallinule.

P. *Martinicus* (L.). Martinique Gallinule.

(*Limicolæ.*)
inc. Longirostres and Pressirostres; Charadriomorphæ, *pt.*

CHARADRIIDÆ.

Vanellus, *Briss.*
V. cristatus, *Meyer.* Lapwing, Plover, Peewit.

Strepsilas, *Ill.*
= Cinclus, *G. R. G.*, "*Mœhr.*"
S. interpres (*L.*). Turnstone.

Squatarola, *Leach.*
S. Helvetica (*L.*). Grey Plover.
 = cinerea, *Yarr.*

Charadrius, *L.*
= Pluvialis, *Briss.*
C. pluvialis, *L.* Golden Plover.
 = Pluvialis viridis, *Ray.*
C. *fulvus*, Gm. Eastern Golden Plover.

Eudromias, *Brehm.*
E. morinellus (*L.*). Dotterel.

Ægialitis, *Boie.*
inc. Hiaticula, *G. R. G.*, and Ægialophilus, *Gld.*
Æ. hiaticula (*L.*). Ringed Plover.
Æ. Curonica (*Gm.*). Little Ringed Plover.
 = Charadrius minor, *Yarr.*
Æ. Cantiana (*Lath.*). Kentish Plover.
Æ. *vocifera* (L.). Killdeer Plover.

Œdicnemus, *Temm.*

Œ. crepitans, *Temm.* Norfolk Plover, Stone-Curlew.
= Charadrius scolopax, *S. G. Gm.*

Hæmatopus, *L.*

H. ostralegus, *L.* Oyster-catcher, Sea-Pie.

Glareola, Gm.

G. *pratincola*, L. Pratincole.
= *torquata,* Yarr.; *Hirundo pratincola,* L.

Cursorius, Lath.

C. *Gallicus* (Gm.). Courser, Cream-coloured Plover.
= *isabellinus,* Meyer.

SCOLOPACIDÆ.

Calidris, *Cuv.*

C. arenaria (*L.*). Sanderling, Curwillet.

Tringa, *L.*

inc. Pelidna, *Cuv.*; Limnicola, *Koch*; Limnocinclus, *Gld.*; Octodromas, *Gld.*; Ancylocheilus, *Gld.*; and Arquatella, *Gld.*

T. canutus, *L.* Knot, Red Sandpiper.
T. Temminckii, *Leisler.* Temminck's Stint.
T. alpina, *L.* Dunlin, Purre, Ox-eye, Sea-Snipe, Summer-Snipe.
— cinclus, *L.*, var.
= variabilis, *Meyer.*
T. maritima, *Brünn.* Purple Sandpiper.
= striata, *L.*
T. subarquata (*Gld.*). Pygmy Curlew.

T. Schinzii, *Bon.*   Schinz's Sandpiper.
    = fuscicollis, *Vieill.*
T. maculata, Vieill.   Pectoral Sandpiper.
    = *pectoralis*, Say.
T. platyrhyncha, *Temm.*   Broad-billed Sandpiper.
    = pygmæa, *G. R. G.*
T. Wilsoni, Nutt.   American Stint.
    = *pusilla*, Wils.
T. minuta, Leisler.   Little Stint.

Totanus, *Bechst.*

inc. Glottis, *Nilss.*; Actitis, *Boie*; Bartramius, *Less.*; Tryngites, *Cab.*; Actiturus, *Bon.*; Tringoides, *Bon.*; and Helodromas, *Kaup.*

T. hypoleucos (*L.*).   Common Sandpiper.
T. macularius (L.).   Spotted Sandpiper.
T. ochropus (*L.*).   Green Sandpiper.
T. glareola (*Gm.*).   Wood-Sandpiper.
T. calidris (*L.*).   Redshank.
    = Calidris Bellonii, *Aldr.*
T. fuscus (*L.*).   Dusky Sandpiper, Spotted Redshank.
    = Limosa grisea, *Briss.*
T. flavipes (Gm.).   Yellowshank.
T. glottis, *Bechst.*   Greenshank.
    = Scolopax canescens, *Gm.*
T. rufescens, Vieill.   Buff-breasted Sandpiper.
T. solitarius, Wils.   Solitary Sandpiper.
T. Bartramii, Wils.   Bartram's Sandpiper.
    = *Bartramia longicauda*, Howard Saunders.

Machetes, *Cuv.*

= Philomachus, *G. R. G.*, "*Mahr.*"

M. pugnax (*L.*).   Ruff ♂, Reeve ♀.
    = Avis pugnax, *Aldr.*

E

Phalaropus, *Briss.*
inc. Lobipes, *Cuv.*

P. lobatus (*L.*).   Grey Phalarope.
= Tringa fulicaria, *L.*

P. hyperboreus (*L.*).   Red-necked Phalarope.

Limosa, *Bechst.*

L. ægocephala (*L.*).   Black-tailed Godwit.
= melanura, *Bechst.*

L. Lapponica (*L.*).   Bar-tailed Godwit.
= rufa, *Temm.*, " *Briss.*"

Himantopus, Briss.
= *Hypsibates*, Nitzsch.

H. candidus, Bonn.   Black-winged Stilt.
= *melanopterus*, Temm.

Numenius, *Briss.*

N. arquata (*L.*).   Curlew.
N. phæopus (*L.*).   Whimbrel, Summer Curlew.
N. borealis (Forst.).   Esquimaux Curlew.

Recurvirostra, *L.*

R. avocetta, *L.*   Avocet, Cobbler's-Awl.

Scolopax, *L.*

S. rusticula, *L.*   Woodcock.
= Gallina rustica, *Gesn.*

Gallinago, *Leach.*
inc. Limnocryptes, *Kaup*; Philolimnus, *Brehm*; and Xylocota, *Bon.*

G. major (*Gm.*).   Great Snipe.

G. gallinaria (*Gm.*). Snipe, Heather-Blite.
  = media, *Gray*; = cœlestis, *Fenzel.*
[G. Sabini (*Vig.*) is a dark variety.]
G. gallinula (*L.*). Jack Snipe.
G. *Brehmii*, Kaup. Brehm's Snipe.
G. *Wilsoni*, Temm. Wilson's Snipe.

Macrorhamphus, Leach.
M. *griseus* (Gm.). Brown Snipe.

(*Herodiones.*)
Cultrirostres, *pt.*; = Pelargomorphæ.

TANTALIDÆ.

Falcinellus, Bechst.
  = *Plegadis*, Kaup.
F. *igneus* (Gm.). Glossy Ibis.

Platalea, L.
  = *Platea*, Briss.
P. *leucorodia*, L. Spoonbill.

CICONIIDÆ.

Ciconia, Briss.
C. *alba*, Bechst., "Will." Stork.
C. *nigra* (L.), "Gesn." Black Stork.

ARDEIDÆ.

Nycticorax, Steph.
N. *griseus* (L.). Night-Heron.
N. *violaceus* (L.). Cayenne Night-Heron.

Botaurus, *Steph.*
inc. Ardetta, G. R. G.

B. stellaris (*L.*). Bittern.
= Ardea botaurus, *Briss.*
B. lentiginosus (*Mont.*). American Bittern.
B. minutus (*L.*). Little Bittern.

Ardea, *L.*
inc. Egretta, *Briss.*; Herodias, *Boie*; Ardeola, *Boie*; Bubulcus, *Gld.*; and Buphus, G. R. G.

A. cinerea, *L.* Heron.
A. purpurea, L. Purple Heron.
A. alba, L. White Heron.
A. garzetta, L. Egret.
A. russata, Wagl. Buff-backed Heron.
= *bubulcus*, Aud.
A. comata, Pall. Squacco Heron.
= *ralloides*, Scop.

NATATORES.
= Anseres and Palmipedes.

Lamellirostres.

Chenomorphæ, *pt.*; *inc.* Amphimorphæ and Odontoglossæ.

PHŒNICOPTERIDÆ.
Phœnicopterus, L.

P. ruber, L. Flamingo.

ANATIDÆ.
Cygnus, *Bechst.*
inc. Olor, *Wagl.*

C. olor (*Gm.*). Mute Swan.

C. musicus, *Bechst.* Wild Swan, Whooper or Hooper, Whistling Swan.
  = ferus, *Leach*; = Anas cygnus, *L.*
C. immutabilis, *Yarr.* Polish Swan.
C. *Americanus*, Sharpless. American Swan.
C. *buccinator*, Rich. Trumpeter Swan.
C. Bewickii, *Yarr.* Bewick's Swan.

Anser, *Briss.*
inc. Chen, *Boie*; and Cygnopsis, *Brandt.*

A. ferus (*Gm.*), "*Gesn.*" Wild Goose, Grey Lag Goose.
A. segetum (*Gm.*). Bean-Goose.
A. *brachyrhynchus*, Bail. Pink-footed Goose.
A. albifrons (*Gm.*). White-fronted Goose.
A. *cygnoides* (L.). Chinese Goose.
A. *Indicus* (Lath.). Bar-headed Goose.
A. *albatus* (Cassin). Snow-Goose.

Bernicla, *Boie.*
inc. Brenta, *Briss.*

B. brenta (*Pall.*). Brent Goose.
B. leucopsis (*Bechst.*). Barnacle Goose.
B. *ruficollis* (Pall.). Red-breasted Goose.
B. *Canadensis* (L.). Canada Goose.

Plectropterus, Steph.
P. *Gambensis* (L.). Spur-winged Goose.

Chenalopex, Steph.
C. *Ægyptiaca* (L.). Egyptian Goose.

Cairina, Flem.
C. *Moschata* (L.). Muscovy Duck.
  = Anas *Cairina*, Aldr.

Tadorna, *Flem.*
inc. Casarca, *Bon.*

T. vulpanser, *Flem.* Sheldrake.
= Anas maritima, *Gesn.*

T. rutila (*Pall.*). Red Duck, Ruddy Duck.
= Anas casarca, *L.*

Rhynchaspis, *Steph.*
= Spatula, *Boie.*

R. clypeata (*L.*). Shoveller.

Anas, *L.*
inc. Chaulelasmus, *G. R. G.*

A. boschas, *L.* Wild Duck, Mallard.
A. strepera, *L.* Gadwall.

Mareca, *Steph.*

M. Penelope (*L.*). Wigeon.
M. *Americana* (Gm.). American Wigeon.

Dafila, *Steph.*

D. acuta (*L.*). Pintail.
= Anas longicauda, *Briss.*

Querquedula, *Steph.*
inc. Nettion, *Kaup*; and Pterocyanea, *G. R. G.*

Q. circia (*L.*). Garganey.
= Anas circia, *Gesn.*

Q. crecca (*L.*). Teal.

[Q. *bimaculata* (K. & B.), = *glocitans* (Pall.), a hybrid between the Teal and Wild Duck.]

Q. *discors* (L.). Blue-winged Teal.
= *Querquedula Virginiana*, Briss.

Q. *Carolinensis* (Gm.). Green-winged Teal.

Æx (*Aix*), Briss.
Æ. sponsa (L.).   Summer Duck.
  = *Anas æstiva*, Briss.

Fuligula, *Steph.*
inc. Glaucium, *Boie*; Branta, *Boie*; Aythya, *Boie*; Nyroca, *Flem.*; and Platypus, *Brehm.*

F. rufina (*Pall.*).   Red-crested Pochard.
F. ferina (*L.*).   Pochard.
F. ferinoides, Bartlett.   American Scaup.
F. marila (*L.*).   Scaup Duck.
  — mariloides, *Yarr.*, var.
F. affinis, Eyton.   Lesser Scaup Duck.
F. cristata (*Leach*).   Tufted Duck.
  = *Anas fuligula*, *L.*
F. collaris (Don.).   Red-necked Duck.
F. ferruginea (*Gm.*).   White-eyed Duck, Red Duck.
  = nyroca, *Yarr.*; leucophthalmus, *Brehm.*

Clangula, *Flem.*
inc. Glaucion, *K. & B.*; Cosmonetta, *Kaup*; and Histrionicus, *Gld.*

C. glaucion (*L.*).   Goldeneye.
C. Islandica (Gm.).   Barrow's Goldeneye.
C. albeola (L).   Buffel-headed Duck.
C. histrionica (L.).   Harlequin Duck.

Harelda, *Steph.*
H. glacialis (*L.*).   Long-tailed Duck.

Heniconetta, G. R. G.
  = *Stelleria*, Bon., and *Polysticta*, Eyton.
H. Stelleri (Pall.).   Steller's Duck.
  = *Anas dispar*, Sparrm.

Somateria, *Leach.*

S. mollissima (*L.*). Eider Duck.
S. spectabilis (L.). King Eider.

Œdemia, *Flem.*

inc. Melanetta, *Bois,* and Pelionetta, *Kaup.*

Œ. nigra (*L.*). Scoter.
Œ. fusca (*L.*). Velvet Duck.
Œ. perspicillata (L.). Surf-Scoter.

MERGIDÆ.

Mergus, *L.*

inc. Merganser, *Briss.*

M. castor, *L.* Goosander.
= merganser, *L.*
M. serrator, *L.* Red-breasted Merganser.
M. cucullatus, L. Hooded Merganser.
M. albellus, *L.* Smew, White Nun.
= Albellus aquaticus, *Aldr.*

(*Steganopodes.*)

= Totipalmatæ and Dysporomorphæ.

PELECANIDÆ.

Sula, *Briss.*, "*Ray.*"

= Dysporus, *Ill.*, and Morus, *Vieill.*

S. Bassana (*L.*). Gannet, Solan Goose.
= alba, *Temm.*; = Anser Bassanus, *Gesn.*

Phalacrocorax, *Briss.*

= Graculus, *L.*; Halieus, *Ill.*; Carbo, *Lac.*; and Hydrocorax, *Vieill.*

P. carbo (*L.*). Cormorant.
= Carbo aquaticus, *Gesn.*

P. graculus (*L.*). Shag.
   = cristatus, *Horting.*

Pelecanus, L.
P. onocrotalus, L. Pelican.

Plotus, L.
P. anhinga, L. Darter, Snake-bird.

(*Tubinares.*)
Cecomorphæ, *pt.*

PROCELLARIIDÆ.

Procellaria, *L.*
   = Thalassidroma, *Vig.*; *inc.* Oceanites, *K. & B.*, and Bulweria, *Bon.*
P. pelagica, *L.* Storm-Petrel, Mother Carey's Chicken.
P. Leachii, *Temm.* Fork-tailed Petrel.
   = leucorrhoa, *Vieill.*
P. Bulweri, Jard. & S. Bulwer's Petrel.
P. oceanica, Kuhl. Wilson's Petrel.
   = *Oceanites oceanicus*, Dresser.

Fulmarus, *Steph.*
   inc. Œstrelata, *Bon.*
F. glacialis (*L.*). Fulmar.
   = Vagellus Cornubiensium, *Ray.*
F. hæsitatus (Kuhl). White-capped Petrel.

Puffinus, *Briss.*
P. Anglorum, *Temm.*, "*Will.*" Manx Shearwater.
   = Diomedea avis, *Gesn.*
P. major, *Faber.* Greater Shearwater, Mollymock.
   = cinereus, *K. & B.*
P. griseus (*Gm.*). Sooty Shearwater.
P. obscurus (Gm.). Dusky Shearwater.

Daption, Steph.

D. capense (L.). Cape Pigeon.
= *Procellaria nævia*, Briss.

Longipennes.
= Gaviæ; Ceoomorphæ, *pt.*

LARIDÆ.
Lestris, *Ill.*
= Stercorarius, *Briss.*

L. catarrhactes (*L.*). Common Skua.
= Skua Hoyeri, *Ray.*

L. pomatorhinus, *Temm.* Pomatorhine Skua.

L. parasiticus (*L.*). Buffon's Skua.

L. crepidatus (*Gm.*). Arctic Skua.

Larus, *L.*
inc. Gavia, *Bois*; Chroicocephalus, *Eyton*; and Hydrocolœus, *Kaup.*

L. canus, *L.* Common Gull, Sea-mew.
= Gavia cinerea, *Briss.*

L. argentatus, *Gm.* Herring-Gull.

L. fuscus, *L.* Lesser Black-backed Gull.

L. marinus, *L.* Greater Black-backed Gull.

L. leucopterus, *Faber.* Iceland Gull.
= Icelandicus, *Flem.*

L. glaucus, *Fabr.* Glaucous Gull.

L. ichthyaëtus, Pall. Great Black-headed Gull.

L. melanocephalus, Nutt. Adriatic Gull.

L. ridibundus, *L.* Black-headed Gull.
= capistratus, *Temm.*

L. atricilla, *L.* Laughing Gull.
= Cephus Turneri, *Gem.*

L. Philadelphiæ, Ord. Bonaparte's Gull.

L. minutus, Pall. Little Gull.

Pagophila, Kaup.
= *Cetosparactes*, MacG.

P. *eburnea*, Phipps.   Ivory Gull.

Rissa, *Steph.*
R. tridactyla (*L.*).   Kittiwake.

Rhodostethia, MacG.
R. *Rossii*, MacG.   Cuneate-tailed Gull.
= *Larus roseus*, MacG.

Xema, J. Ross.
X. *Sabinii*, J. Ross.   Sabine's Gull.

Sterna, *L.*
inc. Hydrochelidon, *Boie*; Gelochelidon, *Boie*; Stylochelidon, *Boie*.
= Hydroprogne, *Gld.*; Actochelidon, *Boie*; Sternula, *Boie*;
and Pelodes, *Kaup.*

S. hirundo, *L.*   Common Tern, Sea-Swallow.
   = fluviatilis, *Naum.*; = Hirundo marina, *Will.*
S. arctica, *Temm.*   Arctic Tern.
   = macrura, *Naum.*
S. Cantiaca, *Gm.*   Sandwich Tern.
S. Dougallii, *Mont.*   Roseate Tern.
S. minuta, *L.*   Lesser Tern.
   = Larus piscator, *Gesn.*
S. Anglica, *Mont.*   Gull-billed Tern.
S. *Caspia*, Pall.   Caspian Tern.
S. *fuliginosa*, Gm.   Sooty Tern.
S. *anæstheta*, Scop.   Small Sooty Tern.
S. nigra, *L.*   Black Tern.
   = fissipes, *Penn.*

S. leucoptera, Schinz.   White-winged Black Tern.
S. hybrida, Pall.   Whiskered Tern.
   = *leucopareia*, Nutt.
[*S. Bergii*, Licht. (=*velox*, Rüppell), erroneously reported.]

Anous, Steph.
   = *Megalopterus*, Boie.
A. stolidus (L.).   Noddy.
   = *Passer stultus*, Will.

(*Pygopodes.*)
   = Brevipennes and Impennes; Ceœomorphæ, *pt.*

COLYMBIDÆ.

Colymbus, *L.*
   = Eudytes, *Ill.*
C. glacialis, *L.*   Great Northern Diver.
C. arcticus, *L.*   Black-throated Diver.
C. septentrionalis, *L.*   Red-throated Diver.

Podiceps, *Lath.*
   inc. Tachybaptes, *Reich.*, and Sylbeocyclus, *Bon.*
P. cristatus (*L.*).   Great Crested Grebe.
P. rubricollis (*Gm.*).   Red-necked Grebe.
P. auritus (*L.*).   Sclavonian Grebe.
   = cornutus, *Auct. Br.*
P. nigricollis, *Brehm.*
   = auritus, *Auct. Br.*
P. minor (*Gm.*).   Dabchick, Little Grebe.

Podilymbus, Less.
P. podiceps (L.).   Pied-billed Grebe.

ALCIDÆ.
Alca, *L.*
inc. Utamania, *Steph.*

A. torda, *L.* Razorbill.

[A. impennis, *L.* Great Auk, Gare-fowl. Probably extinct.]

Uria, *Ill.*
inc. Grylle, *Brandt,* and Lomvia, *Brandt.*

U. troile (*L.*). Guillemot, Willock, Murre.
= lacrymans, *Temm.,* var.

U. Brünnichii, Sabine. Thick-billed Guillemot.

U. grylle (*L.*). Black Guillemot.

Fratercula, *Briss.*
= Mormon, *Ill.*

F. arctica (*L.*). Puffin, Pope, Coulterneb, Scraber, Sea-Parrot.
= Puffinus Anglicus, *Gesn.*

Mergulus, *Vieill.*
= Arctica, *G. R. G.,* "*Mœhr.,*" and Cephus, *Cuv.*

M. alle (*L.*). Little Auk, Rotche.
= melanoleucos, *Flem.*

ACCIPITRES.
= Raptores and Aëtomorphæ.

VULTURIDÆ.
Neophron, Sav.
N. percnopterus (L.). Egyptian Vulture.

Gyps, Sav.
G. fulvus (Gm.). Griffon Vulture.

FALCONIDÆ.

Astur, *Briss.*

A. palumbarius (*L.*), "*Ray.*"   Goshawk.
A. atricapillus, Wils.   Black-capped Hawk.

Accipiter, *Briss.*

A. nisus (*L.*).   Sparrow-Hawk.
= fringillarius, *Gesn.*

Nauclerus, Vig.
= *Elanoides*, Vieill.
N. furcatus (L.).   Swallow-tailed Kite.

Elanus, Sav.
E. cæruleus (Desf.).   Black-winged Kite.

Milvus, *Cuv.*

M. ictinus, *Sav.*   Kite, Glead or Gled.
= regalis, *Briss.*
M. migrans (Bodd.).   Black Kite.

Pernis, *Cuv.*

P. apivorus (*L.*).   Honey-Buzzard.

Buteo, *Lac.*
inc. Archibuteo, *Brehm.*

B. vulgaris, *Leach*, "*Will.*"   Buzzard.
B. borealis (Gm.), "Gesn."   Red-tailed Buzzard.
B. desertorum (Daud.).   African Buzzard.
B. lineatus (Gm.).   Red-shouldered Buzzard.
B. lagopus (L.).   Rough-legged Buzzard.

Circus, *Lac.*

C. cyaneus (*L.*). Hen-Harrier.
C. cineraceus (*Mont.*). Montagu's Harrier.
C. æruginosus (*L.*). Moor-Buzzard, Marsh-Harrier.
= Milvus æruginosus, *Aldr.*

Pandion, *Sav.*

P. haliaëtus (*L.*). Osprey.

Aquila, *Briss.*

A. chrysaëtus (*L.*), "*Will.*" Golden Eagle.
A. nævia (Gm.). Spotted Eagle.

Haliaëtus, *Sav.*

H. albicilla (*L.*). Erne, White-tailed Eagle.

Falco, *L.*

inc. Hierofalco, *Cuv.*; Tinnunculus, *Vieill.*; Cerchneis, *Boie*; Hypotriorchis, *Boie*; and Erythropus, *Gld.*

F. gyrfalco, *L.* Gyr Falcon.
F. candicans, *Gm.* Greenland Falcon.
F. islandicus, *Gm.* Iceland Falcon.
F. peregrinus, *Gm.* Peregrine Falcon.
F. subbuteo, *L.* Hobby.
F. æsalon, *L.* Merlin.
F. innunculus, *L.* Kestrel, Windhover.
= Tinnunculus accipiter, *Gesn.*
F. cenchris, Naum. Lesser Kestrel.
F. vespertinus, L. Red-footed Falcon.
= *rufipes*, Temm.

STRIGIDÆ.

Athene, Boie.
= *Noctua,* Sav.; *Glaucidium,* Boie; and *Carine,* Kaup.

A. passerina (L.). Little Owl.
= Noctua minima, *Gesn.*

Nyctale, Brehm.
N. Tengmalmi (Gm.). Tengmalm's Owl.
N. Acadica (Gm.). Sparrow-Owl.

Nyctea, Steph.
N. nivea (Daud.). Snowy Owl.
= *Strix nyctea,* L.; *Scandiaca,* Newton.

Surnia, Dum.
S. ulula (L.). Hawk-Owl.
S. funerea (L.). American Hawk-Owl.

Otus, *Cuv.*
= Asio, *Briss.*; *inc.* Brachyotus, *Gld.*

O. vulgaris, *Flem.* Long-eared Owl.
= Bubo asio, *Briss.*

O. brachyotus, *Forst.* Short-eared Owl.
= Asio accipitrinus, *Newton.*

Scops, Sav.
= *Ephialtes,* G. R. G.

S. Aldrovandi, Flem., "Ray." Little Eared Owl.
= *giu,* Scop.

S. asio (L.). Red Owl, Little Screech Owl.

Bubo, *Cuv.*
B. maximus, *Flem.,* "*Sibbald.*" Great Eagle Owl.
= Strix Scandiaca, *L.*; Strix ignavus, *Forster.*

Syrnium, *Sav.*

S. aluco (*L.*).   Tawny Owl, Ivy-Owl.
= Strix cinerea, *Ray*; Strix stridula, *L.*

Strix, *L.*
= Aluco, *Briss.*

S. flammea, *L.*   Barn-Owl, White Owl.

Class 5. MAMMALIA. (MAMMALS.)

RODENTIA.
= Glires and Rosores.

LEPORIDÆ.

Lepus, *L.*

L. timidus, *L.*   Hare.
L. variabilis, *Pall.*   Alpine Hare.
= Hibernicus, *Yarr.*, var.
L. cuniculus, *L.*   Rabbit, Coney.

MURIDÆ.

Arvicola, *Lac.*

A. amphibius (*L.*).   Water-Rat, Water-Vole.
A. agrestis (*L.*).   Field-Mouse, Field-Vole.
A. pratensis, *Baillon.*   Bank-Vole.
= riparius, *Yarr.*; rufescens, *De Selys.*

Mus, *L.*

M. sylvaticus, *L.*   Wood-Mouse.
M. messorius, *Shaw.*   Harvest-Mouse.

M. musculus, *L.*   Common Mouse.
M. rattus, *L.*   Black Rat.
M. decumanus, *Pall.*   Brown Rat.

MYOXIDÆ.

Myoxus, *Schreb.*

M. avellanarius (*L.*).   Dormouse.
= Mus avellanarius, *L.*

SCIURIDÆ.

Sciurus, *L.*

S. vulgaris, *L.*   Squirrel.

CHIROPTERA.

VESPERTILIONIDÆ.
Primates, *pt.*; = Volitantia.

Plecotus, *Geoff.*

P. auritus (*L.*).   Long-eared Bat.
= brevimanus, *Jenyns.*

Synotus, *K. & B.*
= Barbastellus, *Gray.*

S. barbastellus, *Schreb.*   Barbastelle.

Vespertilio, *L.*

V. murinus, *Schreb.*
V. Bechsteinii, *Leisler.*
V. Nattereri, *Kuhl.*
V. emarginatus, *Geoff.*
V. Daubentonii, *Leisler.*
V. mystacinus, *Leisler.*

Vesperugo, *K. & B.*

V. pipistrellus (*Schreb.*). Common Bat, Flitter-Mouse.
 = Vespertilio pygmæus, *Leach*.
V. Leisleri, *Kuhl.*
V. discolor, *Natterer.*
V. noctula, *Schreb.* Great Bat.
 = Vespertilio altivolans, *G. White* (Selborne).
V. serotinus, *Schreb.*

Rhinolophus, *Geoff.*

R. ferrum-equinum (*Schreb.*). Greater Horseshoe Bat.
R. hipposideros (*Bechst.*). Lesser Horseshoe Bat.

INSECTIVORA.

TALPIDÆ.

Talpa, *L.*

T. Europæa, *L.* Mole, Want.

SORICIDÆ.

Sorex, *L.*

S. araneus, *L.* Shrew, Shrew-Mouse.
 = Mus araneus, *Gesn.*

Crossopus, *Wagl.*

C. fodiens (*Schreb.*). Water-Shrew.
C. remipes (*Geoff.*). Oared Shrew.

ERINACEIDÆ.

Erinaceus, *L.*

E. Europæus, *L.* Hedgehog, Urchin.
 = terrestris, *Gesn.*

UNGULATA.

= Pecora; *inc.* Ruminantia *or* Selenodontia.

CERVIDÆ.

Cervus, *L.*

C. elaphus, *L.*   Red Deer, Stag, Hart ♂, Hind ♀.

Dama, *H. Smith.*

D. vulgaris, *Brookes,* "*Gesn.*"   Fallow Deer, Buck ♂, Doe ♀, Fawn *young.*
D. capreolus (*L.*).   Roebuck.

CETACEA.

BALÆNOPTERIDÆ.

Balænoptera, *Lac.*
inc. Physalis, *Flem.*

B. boops (*L.*).   Fin-fish, Finner, Rorqual, Razorback.
= Balæna musculus, *L.*

Balæna, *L.*

B. mysticetus, *L.*   Common Whale, Greenland Whale.

PHYSETERIDÆ.

Physeter, *L.*

P. macrocephalus, *L.*   Sperm-Whale, Cachalot.
P. tursio, *L.*   High-finned Cachalot.

MONODONTIDÆ.

Monodon, *L.*

M. monoceros, *L.*   Narwhal, Sea-Unicorn.
= Monoceros piscis, *Will.*

HYPEROODONTIDÆ.

Hyperoodon, *Lac.*

H. bidens (*Schreb.*). Bottlehead.
= Delphinus hyperoodon, *Desmarest.*

Ziphius, *Gray.*
= *Diodon*, Lesson.

Z. bidens (Sowerby). Sowerby's Whale.
= *Sowerbyensis*, Gray.

DELPHINIDÆ.

Delphinus, *L.*

D. delphis, *L.* Dolphin.
D. tursio, *Fabr.* Bottlenose Dolphin.
= truncatus, *Mont.*

Orca, *Gray.*

O. gladiator (*Bonn.*). Grampus.
= Delphinus orca, *L.*

Phocæna, *Cuv.*

P. communis, *Less.* Porpoise, Sea-Hog, Hog-fish.
= Delphinus phocæna, *L.*

Globiocephalus, *Gray.*

G. melas (*Trail*). Ca'ing Whale, Round-headed Porpoise.
= Delphinus globiceps, *Cuv.*

Beluga, *Gray.*

B. leucas (*Pall.*). White Whale, White-fish.
= Delphinus albicans, *Fabr.*

PINNIPEDIA.

PHOCIDÆ.

Halichœrus, Nilss.

H. gryphus, Fabr.   Grey Seal.
= griseus, *Nilss.*

Phoca, *L.*

P. vitulina, *L.*   Common Seal, Sea-calf.
P. Groënlandica, *Müll.*   Harp Seal.
P. barbata, *Müll.*   Great Seal.

Trichechus, L.

T. rosmarus, *L.*   Walrus, Morse, Sea-Cow.

CARNIVORA.
= Feræ.

MUSTELIDÆ.

Putorius, *Cuv.*

P. vulgaris, *Rich.*, "*Briss.*"   Weasel.
P. erminea (*L.*).   Stoat, Greater Weasel, Ermine.
P. fetidus, *Gray.*   Polecat, Fitchet.
 [P. furo (*L.*).   Ferret, var.]

Mustela, *L.*

M. martes, *L.*   Marten, Pine-Marten.
= foina, *Gm.*; Martes abietum, *Ray.*

Meles, *Storr.*

M. taxus, *Pall.*   Badger.
= Ursus meles, *L.*

Lutra, *Storr.*

L. vulgaris, *Erxleben.* Otter.
= Mustela lutra, *L.*
— Roensis, *Ogilby*, var.

CANIDÆ.

[*Canis*, L.

C. *latrans*, Say. Prairie-Dog. Introduced.]

Vulpes, *Briss.*

V. vulgaris, *Briss.* Fox.
= Canis vulpes, *L.*

FELIDÆ.

Felis, *L.*

F. catus, *L.* Wild Cat.

ADDITION AND CORRECTIONS.

Page 11, *after* Lepadogaster Gouani, *Risso*, *add* = Cornubiensis, *Flem.*
 ,,   ,, *for* bimaculatus (*Penn.*) *read* bimaculata, *Flem.*
 ,, 40, *E. schœniclus* should be in Roman type.
 ,, 58, line 25, and page 60, line 3, *for* Nutt. *read* Natt.

INDEX.

Aberdevine, 39.
Abramis, 3.
Acanthias, 23.
Acantholabrus, 10.
Acanthopterygii, 11.
Acanthyllis, 32.
Accentor, 36.
Accipiter, 62.
Accipitres, 61.
Acerina, 19.
Acipenser, 25.
Acipenseridæ, 25.
Acrania. 1.
Acredula, 38.
Acrocephalus, 34.
Actitis, 49.
Actiturus, 49.
Actochelidon, 59.
Adder, 27.
Aëdon, 35.
Ægialitis, 47.
Ægialophilus, 47.
Ægiothus, 40.
Aëtomorphæ, 61.
Æx, 55.
Agelæus, 42.
Agonus, 17.
Aix, 55.
Alauda, 41.
Alaudidæ, 41.
Alausa, 2.
Albacore, 15.
Alburnus, 3.

Alca, 61.
Alcedinidæ, 30.
Alcedo, 30.
Alcidæ, 61.
Alectorides, 45.
Alectoromorphæ, 43.
Alopecias, 24.
Alosa, 2.
Ammocœtes, 1.
Ammodytes, 8.
Ampelidæ, 41.
Ampelis, 41.
Amphibia, 26.
Amphimorphæ, 52.
Amphioxidæ, 1.
Amphioxus, 1.
Anacanthini, 6.
Anarrhicas, 12.
Anas, 54.
Anatidæ, 52.
Anchovy, 3.
Ancylocheilus, 48.
Andalusian Quail, 44.
Angel-fish, 23.
Angler, 13.
Anguilla, 2.
Anguis, 28.
Anorthura, 38.
Anous, 60.
Anser, 53.
Anseres, 52.

Anthropoides, 45.
Anthus, 37.
Aphia, 14.
Apternus, 29.
Aquila, 63.
Archibuteo, 62.
Arctica, 61.
Ardea, 52.
Ardeidæ, 51.
Ardeola, 52.
Ardetta, 52.
Argentina, 5.
Argentine, 5, 6.
Argyropelecus, 6.
Arnoglossus, 7.
Arquatella, 48.
Arvicola, 65.
Asio, 64.
Aspidophorus, 17.
Astur, 62.
Athene, 64.
Atherina, 11.
Auk, 61.
Auxis, 15.
Aves, 29.
Avocet, 50.
Aythya, 55.

Badger, 70.
Balæna, 68.
Balænidæ, 68.
Balænoptera, 68.
Balænopteridæ, 68.

Balearica, 45.
Balistes, 21.
Balistidæ, 21.
Band-fish, 11.
Barbastellus, 66.
Barbel, 3.
Barbus, 3.
Barnacle Goose, 53.
Bartramia, 49.
Bartramius, 49.
Basse, 19.
Bat, 67.
Batoidei, 21.
Batrachia, 26.
Bean-Goose, 53.
Bearded Tit, 38.
Beardie, 3.
Becker, 18.
Bee-eater, 30.
Belone, 4.
Beluga, 69.
Bergylt, 18.
Bernicla, 53.
Bib, 9.
Birds, 29.
Bittern, 52.
Black Basse, 19.
Blackbird, 36.
Blackcap, 34.
Black-fish, 16.
Black Grouse, 44.
Blade-fish, 17.
Bleak, 3.
Blenniidæ, 12.
Blenniops, 12.
Blennius, 12.
Blenny, 12.
Blindworm, 28.
Blue Poll, 5.
Blue Shark, 24.
Bluethroat, 35.
Boar-fish, 15.

Bogue, 18.
Bombycilla, 41.
Bone-dog, 23.
Bonito, 15.
Borer, 1.
Botaurus, 52.
Botia, 3.
Bottlehead, 69.
Bottle-tom, 38.
Bounce, 24.
Box, 18.
Brachyotus, 64.
Bradypterus, 34.
Braize, 18.
Brama, 16.
Brambling, 39.
Branchiostoma, 1.
Branta, 55.
Bream, 3, 18, 19.
Brenta, 53.
Brent Goose, 53.
Brett, 6.
Brevipennes, 60.
Brill, 6.
Brook-Trout, 5.
Brosmius, 9.
Browny, 7.
Bubo, 64.
Bubulcus, 52.
Buck, 68.
Budytes, 37.
Bufo, 26.
Bufonidæ, 26.
Bulbul, 36.
Bullcod, 12.
Bullfinch, 39.
Bullhead, 17.
Bulweria, 57.
Bunting, 40.
Buphus, 52.
Burbot, 8.
Bustard, 45.
Butalis, 33.
Butcher-bird, 33.

Buteo, 62.
Butt, 7.
Butter-fish, 12.
Buzzard, 62.

Caccabis, 44.
Cachalot, 68.
Ca'ing Whale, 69.
Cairina, 53.
Calamodus, 34.
Calamodyta, 34.
Calamoherpe, 34.
Calamophilus, 38.
Calandra Lark, 41.
Calandrella, 41.
Calcarius, 40.
Calidris, 48.
Callionymus, 14.
Canary, 40.
Canidæ, 71.
Canis, 71.
Cantharus, 19.
Cape Pigeon, 58.
Capercailie, 44.
Caprimulgidæ, 31.
Caprimulgus, 31.
Capros, 15.
Carangidæ, 14.
Caranx, 14.
Carassius, 4.
Carbo, 56.
Carcharias, 24.
Carchariidæ, 24.
Carduelis, 39.
Carelophus, 12.
Carine, 64.
Carnivora, 70.
Carp, 4.
Carpodacus, 39.
Carrion-Crow, 42.
Carter, 7.
Caryocatactes, 43.

INDEX. 75

Casarca, 54.
Cat, 71.
Cat-fish, 12.
Cecomorphæ, 57, 58, 60.
Cedar-bird, 41.
Centrina, 23.
Centriscidæ, 11.
Centriscus, 11.
Centrolabrus, 10.
Centrolophus, 16.
Centronotus, 12, 14.
Centrophanes, 40.
Cephaloptera, 22.
Cephus, 61.
Cepola, 11.
Cepolidæ, 11.
Cerchneis, 63.
Certhia, 32.
Certhiidæ, 32.
Cervidæ, 68.
Cervus, 68.
Ceryle, 30.
Cetacea, 68.
Cetosparactes, 59.
Cettia, 34.
Chad, 18.
Chætura, 32.
Chaffinch, 39.
Charadriidæ, 47.
Charadriomorphæ, 47.
Charadrius, 47, 48.
Charr, 5, 6.
Chaulelasmus, 54.
Chelidon, 31.
Chelonia, 28.
Cheloniidæ, 28.
Chen, 53.
Chenalopex, 53.
Chenomorphæ, 52.

Chiffchaff, 34.
Chimæra, 25.
Chimæridæ, 25.
Chiroptera, 66.
Chondropterygii, 21.
Chough, 43.
Chroicocephalus, 58.
Chrysomitris, 39.
Chrysophrys, 18.
Chub, 3.
Ciconia, 51.
Ciconiidæ, 51.
Ciliata, 9.
Cinclidæ, 37.
Cinclus, 37, 47.
Circus, 63.
Cirl-Bunting, 40.
Citril Finch, 39.
Clamatores, 43.
Clangula, 55.
Clupea, 2.
Clupeidæ, 2.
Coal-fish, 9.
Cobbler's-awl, 50.
Cobitis, 3.
Coccothraustes, 39.
Coccyges, 32.
Coccygomorphæ, 30, 32.
Coccystes, 32.
Coccyzus, 32.
Cock-paddle, 13.
Cod, 9.
Colaptes, 29.
Cole-Mouse, 38.
Coleomorphæ, 29.
Coluber, 27.
Colubridæ, 27.
Columba, 43.
Columbæ, 43.
Columbidæ, 43.

Colymbidæ, 60.
Colymbus, 60.
Comber, 19.
Coney, 65.
Conger, 2.
Conirostres, 32.
Connor, 10.
Cook, 10.
Coot, 46.
Copper-Finch, 39.
Coracias, 30, 41.
Coraciidæ, 30.
Coracomorphæ, 32.
Coregonus, 5.
Coris, 10.
Coriudo, 28.
Corkling, 10.
Corkwing, 10.
Cormorant, 56.
Corn-Crake, 46.
Cornix, 30.
Coronella, 27.
Corvidæ, 42.
Corvus, 42.
Coryphænidæ, 16.
Coryphænoides, 8.
Corythus, 39.
Cosmonetta, 55.
Cotile, 31.
Cottus, 18.
Coturnix, 44.
Couchia, 9.
Coulterneb, 61.
Courser, 48.
Crake, 46.
Cramp Ray, 23.
Crane, 45.
Creeper, 32.
Crenilabrus, 10.
Crex, 46.
Crithagra, 39.
Crithophaga, 40.

G 2

Crossbill, 38.
Crossopus, 67.
Crouger, 4.
Crow, 42.
Crystallogobius, 14.
Ctenolabrus, 10.
Cuckoo, 32.
Cuculidæ, 32.
Cuculus, 32.
Cultrirostres, 45, 51.
Curlew, 50.
Cursorius, 48.
Curruca, 33.
Curwillet, 48.
Cushat, 43.
Cyanecula, 35.
Cyclopteridæ, 13.
Cyclopterus, 13.
Cyclostomi, 1.
Cygnopsis, 53.
Cygnus, 52.
Cyprinidæ, 3.
Cyprinus, 4.
Cypselidæ, 31.
Cypselomorphæ, 30.
Cypselus, 31.
Cyttidæ, 16.

Dab, 7.
Dabchick, 60.
Dace, 3.
Dafila, 54.
Dalatias, 23.
Dama, 68.
Daption, 58.
Darter, 57.
Dartford Warbler, 35.
Dasybatis, 21.
Daulias, 35.
Deal-fish, 12.

Deer, 68.
Delphinidæ, 69.
Delphinus, 69.
Demoiselle, 45.
Dendrocopus, 29.
Dentex, 19.
Dentirostres, 32.
Dicerobatis, 22.
Diodon, 69.
Dipper, 37.
Dishwasher, 37.
Diver, 60.
Doe, 68.
Dog-fish, 23.
Dolphin, 69.
Dor-Hawk, 31.
Dormouse, 66.
Dorsch, 9.
Dory, 16.
Dotterel, 47.
Dove, 43.
Dryocopus, 29.
Duck, 54.
Dunlin, 48.
Dysporomorphæ, 56.
Dysporus, 56.

Eagle, 63.
Eagle-Owl, 64.
Eagle-Ray, 22.
Echeneis, 15.
Echinorhinus, 23.
Echiodon, 8.
Ectopistes, 43.
Eel, 2.
Eel-Pout, 8, 13.
Eft, 26.
Egret, 52.
Egretta, 52.
Eider, 56.
Elanoides, 62.
Elanus, 62.

Elasmobranchii, 21.
Emberiza, 40.
Engraulis, 3.
Eniconetta, *see* Heniconetta.
Enneoctonus, 33.
Ephialtes, 64.
Erinaceidæ, 67.
Erinaceus, 67.
Erithacus, 35.
Ermine, 70.
Erne, 63.
Erythropus, 63.
Erythrosterna, 33.
Esocidæ, 4.
Esox, 4.
Eudromias, 47.
Eudytes, 60.
Eupodotis, 45.
Euspiza, 40.
Exocœtus, 4.

Falcinellus, 51.
Falco, 63.
Falcon, 63.
Falconidæ, 62.
Fallow Deer, 68.
Father-lasher, 18.
Fawn, 68.
Felidæ, 71.
Felis, 71.
Feræ, 70.
Fern-Owl, 31.
Ferret, 70.
Ficedula, 34.
Fieldfare, 36.
Field-Mouse, 65.
Fierasfer, 8.
File-fish, 21.
Finch, 38.
Fin-fish, 68.
Finner, 68.
Fishes, 1.

INDEX.

Fishing-frog, 13.
Fissirostres, 30.
Fitchet, 70.
Flamingo, 52.
Flitter-Mouse, 67.
Flounder, 7.
Fluke, 7.
Flusher, 33.
Flycatcher, 33.
Flying-fish, 4.
Forkbeard, 9.
Fox, 71.
Fox-Shark, 24.
Fratercula, 61.
Fregilus, 43.
Fringilla, 39.
Fringillidæ, 38.
Frog, 26.
Frog-fish, 13.
Fruticicola, 35.
Fulica, 46.
Fulicariæ, 46.
Fuligula, 55.
Fulmar, 57.
Fulmarus, 57.

Gadidæ, 8.
Gadus, 9.
Gadwall, 54.
Galerita, 41.
Galeus, 25.
Gallinæ, 43.
Gallinago, 50.
Gallinula, 46.
Gannet, 56.
Ganoidei, 25.
Gare-fowl, 61.
Garganey, 54.
Garpike, 4.
Garrulus, 42.
Garvie, 2.
Gastrobranchus, 1.
Gastrosteidæ, 20.
Gastrosteus, 20.

Gavia, 58.
Gaviæ, 58.
Gecinus, 29.
Gedd, 4.
Gelochelidon, 59.
Gemitores, 43.
Geranomorphæ, 45, 46.
Gilthead, 10.
Glareola, 48.
Glaucidium, 64.
Glaucion, 55.
Glaucium, 55.
Glead, 62.
Glires, 65.
Globe-fish, 21.
Globiocephalus, 69.
Glottis, 49.
Glut, 2.
Glycyspina, 40.
Goatsucker, 31.
Gobiesocidæ, 11.
Gobiidæ, 13.
Gobio, 4.
Gobiosoma, 14.
Gobius, 13.
Goby, 13.
Godwit, 50.
Golden-crested Wren, 35.
Golden Eagle, 63.
Goldeneye, 55.
Golden Oriole, 41.
Golden Plover, 47.
Goldfinch, 39.
Goldfish, 4.
Goldsinny, 10.
Goosander, 56.
Goose, 53.
Goshawk, 62.
Gowdie, 14.
Gowk, 32.
Grackle, 42.

Gracula, 42.
Graculus, 43.
Graining, 3.
Grallæ, 45.
Grallatores, 45.
Grampus, 69.
Grasshopper Warbler, 34.
Grayling, 5.
Grebe, 60.
Greenbone, 4.
Greenfinch, 39.
Greenland Shark, 23.
Greenshank, 49.
Grey, 5.
Greybird, 36.
Grey Mullet, 11.
Grey Plover, 47.
Grey Seal, 70.
Griffon Vulture, 61.
Grig, 2.
Grilse, 5.
Grosbeak, 39.
Groundling, 3.
Grouse, 44.
Gruidæ, 45.
Grus, 45.
Grylle, 61.
Gudgeon, 4.
Guffer, 13.
Guillemot, 61.
Gull, 58.
Gunnel-fish, 12.
Gunnellus, 12.
Gurnard, 17.
Gwyniad, 5.
Gymnetrus, 12.
Gymnodontes, 21.
Gyps, 61.
Gyrfalcon, 63.

Haddock, 9.

INDEX.

Hæmatopus, 48.
Hæmatornis, 36.
Hag, 1.
Hairtail, 17.
Hake, 9.
Haliaëtos, 63.
Halibut, 6.
Halichœrus, 70.
Halieus, 56.
Hammer-headed Shark, 25.
Hare, 65.
Harelda, 55.
Harlequin Duck, 55.
Harrier, 63.
Hart, 68.
Harvest-Mouse, 65.
Hawfinch, 39.
Hawk, 62.
Hawk's-bill Turtle, 28.
Heather-blite, 51.
Hedgehog, 67.
Hedge-Sparrow, 36.
Helodromas, 49.
Hemipodius, 44.
Hen-Harrier, 63.
Heniconetta, 55.
Herodias, 52.
Herodiones, 51.
Heron, 52.
Herring, 2.
Hiaticula, 47.
Hierofalco, 63.
Himantopus, 50.
Hind, 68.
Hippocampidæ, 20.
Hippocampus, 20.
Hippoglossoides, 6.

Hippoglossus, 6.
Hirundinidæ, 31.
Hirundo, 31.
Histrionicus, 55.
Hobby, 63.
Hog-fish, 69.
Holocephali, 25.
Honey-Buzzard, 62.
Hoopoe, 30.
Horse-Mackerel, 14.
Houbara, 45.
House-Martin, 31.
Huro, 19.
Hydrochelidon, 59.
Hydrocolœus, 58.
Hydrocorax, 56.
Hydroprogne, 59.
Hyperoodon, 69.
Hyperoodontidæ, 69.
Hypolais, 34.
Hypotriorchis, 63.
Hypsibates, 50.

Ibis, 51.
Ide, 3.
Impennes, 60.
Insectivora, 67.
Insessores, 30–32.

Jack, 4.
Jackdaw, 42.
Jack Snipe, 51.
Jay, 42.
John Dory, 16.
Julis, 10.
Jyngidæ, 30.
Jynx, 30.

Kelt, 5.
Kestrel, 63.

King Eider, 56.
Kingfisher, 30.
King of the Bream, 18.
King of the Herrings, 35.
Kite, 6, 62.
Kittiwake, 59.
Knot, 48.

Labrax, 19.
Labridæ, 10.
Labrus, 10.
Lacerta, 27.
Lacertidæ, 27.
Lacertilia, 27.
Lady-fluke, 6.
Læmargus, 23.
Lagopus, 44.
Lamellirostres, 52.
Lamna, 24.
Lamnidæ, 24.
Lampern, 1.
Lamprey, 1.
Lampris, 16.
Lancelet, 1.
Land-Rail, 46.
Laniidæ, 33.
Lanius, 33.
Lantern-fish, 7.
Lapwing, 47.
Laridæ, 58.
Lark, 41.
Larus, 58.
Latrunculus, 14.
Launce, 8.
Laverock, 41.
Leathery Turtle, 28.
Lemon Sole, 7.
Lepadogaster, 11.
Lepidopus, 16.
Leporidæ, 65.
Leptocardii, 1.

Leptocephalus, 2.
Lepus, 65.
Lestris, 58.
Leuciscus, 3.
Lichia, 15.
Ligurinus, 39.
Limicolæ, 47.
Limnicola, 48.
Limnocinclus, 48.
Limnocryptes, 50.
Limosa, 50.
Linaria, 40.
Ling, 8.
Linnet, 40.
Linota, 40.
Liparis, 13.
Lissotriton, 26.
Little Auk, 61.
Lizard, 28.
Lobipes, 50.
Loche, 3.
Locustella, 34.
Lomvia, 61.
Long-dab, 6.
Longipennes, 58.
Long-tailed Tit, 38.
Lophiidæ, 13.
Lophius, 13.
Lophobranchii, 20.
Lophophanes, 38.
Lota, 8.
Loxia, 38.
Lumpenus, 12.
Lump-fish, 13.
Luscinia, 35.
Lutra, 71.
Luvarus, 16.

Machetes, 49.
Mackerel, 15.
Mackerel-Midge, 9.

Macrochires, 32.
Macrodactylus, 46.
Macrorhamphus, 51.
Macruridæ, 5.
Magnirostres, 32.
Magpie, 42.
Maigre, 17.
Mailed Gurnard, 17.
Mallard, 54.
Mammalia, 65.
Mareca, 54.
Marsipobranchii, 1.
Marten, 70.
Martin, 31.
Martinique Gallinule, 46.
Mary Sole, 7.
Maurolicus, 6.
Mavis, 36.
Meadow-Lark, 42.
Mecistura, 38.
Megalornis, 45.
Megrim, 7.
Melanetta, 56.
Melanocorypha, 41.
Meles, 70.
Melizophilus, 35.
Merganser, 56.
Mergidæ, 56.
Mergulus, 61.
Mergus, 56.
Merlangus, 9.
Merlin, 63.
Merluccius, 9.
Meropidæ, 30.
Merops, 30.
Miller's Dog, 25.
Miller's Thumb, 18.

Milvus, 62.
Minnow, 3.
Missel-Thrush, 36.
Mole, 67.
Molebut, 31.
Molge, 26.
Mollymock, 57.
Molva, 8.
Monk-fish, 23.
Monochirus, 7.
Monodon, 68.
Monodontidæ, 68.
Monticola, 36.
Moor-Buzzard, 63.
Moorhen, 46.
Morgay, 24.
Mormon, 61.
Morrhua, 9.
Morse, 70.
Morus, 56.
Motacilla, 37.
Motacillidæ, 37.
Motella, 8.
Mother Cary's Chicken, 57.
Mouse, 65.
Mugil, 11.
Mugilidæ, 11.
Mullet, 19.
Mullidæ, 19.
Mullus, 19.
Muræna, 2.
Murænidæ, 2.
Muridæ, 65.
Murre, 61.
Mus, 65.
Muscicapa, 33.
Muscicapidæ, 33.
Muscovy Duck, 53.
Mustela, 70.
Mustelidæ, 70.

Mustelus, 25.
Myliobates, 22.
Myliobatidæ, 22.
Myoxidæ, 66.
Myoxus, 66.
Myxine, 1.

Narwhal, 68.
Natatores, 52.
Natrix, 27.
Natterjack, 26.
Nauclerus, 62.
Naucrates, 14.
Nemachilus, 3.
Neophron, 61.
Nerophis, 20.
Nettion, 54.
Newt, 26.
Night-Heron, 51.
Nightingale, 35.
Nightjar, 31.
Nine-killer, 33.
Noctua, 64.
Noddy, 60.
Norfolk Plover, 48.
Norway Haddock, 18.
Notidanidæ, 24.
Notidanus, 24.
Nucifraga, 43.
Numb-fish, 23.
Numenius, 50.
Nurse-hound, 24.
Nutcracker, 43.
Nuthatch, 32.
Nyctale, 64.
Nyctea, 64.
Nycticorax, 51.
Nyroca, 55.

Oar-fish, 12.
Oceanites, 57.
Octodromas, 48.

Odontoglossæ, 52.
Œdemia, 56.
Œdicnemus, 48.
Œstrelata, 57.
Old Wife, 10.
Olor, 52.
Opah, 16.
Ophidia, 27.
Ophidiidæ, 8.
Ophidium, 8.
Orca, 69.
Orcynus, 15.
Orfe, 3.
Oriole, 41.
Oriolidæ, 41.
Oriolus, 41.
Orites, 38.
Orthagoriscidæ, 21.
Orthagoriscus, 21.
Ortolan, 40.
Ortygometra, 46.
Ortyx, 44.
Oscines, 32.
Osmerus, 5.
Osprey, 63.
Ostracion, 21.
Ostraciontidæ, 21.
Otidæ, 45.
Otis, 45.
Otocorys, 41.
Otter, 71.
Otterpike, 17.
Otus, 64.
Owl, 64.
Ox-eye, 48.
Ox-Ray, 22.
Oxylophus, 32.
Oystercatcher, 48.

Pagellus, 18.
Pagophila, 59.
Pagrus, 18.

Painted Bunting, 40.
Palæichthyes, 21, 25.
Palmipedes, 52.
Palumbus, 43.
Pammelas, 14.
Pandion, 63.
Panurus, 38.
Paralepis, 6.
Paridæ, 38.
Partridge, 44.
Parr, 5.
Parus, 38.
Passenger Pigeon, 43.
Passer, 38, 39.
Passeres, 32.
Pastor, 42.
Pearl, 6.
Peewit, 47.
Pelamys, 15.
Pelargomorphæ, 51.
Pelecanidæ, 56.
Pelecanus, 57.
Pelias, 27.
Pelican, 57.
Pelidna, 48.
Pelionetta, 56.
Pelodes, 59.
Penny-dog, 25.
Perca, 19.
Perch, 19.
Percidæ, 19.
Perdix, 44.
Peregrine Falcon, 63.
Peristedion, 17.
Peristeromorphæ, 43.
Peristethus, 17.
Pernis, 62.
Petrel, 57.

INDEX. 81

Petrocincla, 36.
Petrocossyphus, 36.
Petromyzon, 1.
Petromyzontidæ, 1.
Pettychaps, 34.
Phalacrocorax, 56.
Phalarope, 50.
Phalaropus, 50.
Pharyngobranchii, 1.
Pharyngognathi, 10.
Phasianidæ, 44.
Phasianus, 44.
Pheasant, 44.
Philolimnus, 50.
Philomachus, 49.
Philomela, 35.
Phoca, 70.
Phocæna, 69.
Phocidæ, 70.
Phœnicopteridæ, 52.
Phœnicopterus, 52.
Phrynorhombus, 7.
Phycis, 9.
Phyllopneuste, 34.
Phylloscopus, 34.
Physalis, 68.
Physeter, 68.
Physeteridæ, 68.
Physostomi, 2.
Pica, 42.
Picariæ, 29, 32.
Pici, 29.
Picidæ, 29.
Picked Dog-fish. 23.

Pickerell, 4.
Picoides, 29.
Picus, 29.
Pigeon, 43.
Pike, 4.
Pilchard, 2.
Pilot-fish, 14.
Pine-Grosbeak, 39.
Pine-Marten, 70.
Pinicola, 39.
Pink, 5.
Pinnipedia, 70.
Pintail, 54.
Pipe-fish, 20.
Piper, 17.
Pipit, 37.
Pisces, 1.
Plaice, 7.
Platalea, 51.
Platea, 51.
Platessa, 7.
Platypus, 55.
Plecotus, 66.
Plectognathi, 21.
Plectrophanes, 40.
Plectropterus, 53.
Plegadis, 51.
Pleuronectes, 7.
Pleuronectidæ, 6.
Plotus, 57.
Plover, 47.
Pluvialis, 47.
Pochard, 55.
Podiceps, 60.
Podilymbus, 60.
Pœcile, 38.
Pogge, 17.
Poison-pate, 18.
Pole, 7.
Polecat, 70.
Polewig, 13.
Pollack, 9.
Pollan, 5.

Polyprion, 19.
Polysticta, 55.
Poor-Cod, 9.
Pope, 19, 61.
Porbeagle, 24.
Porphyrio, 46.
Porpoise, 69.
Porzana, 46.
Potamodus, 34.
Potassou, 9.
Powan, 5.
Power-Cod, 9.
Prairie-Wolf, 71.
Pratincola, 35.
Pratincole, 48.
Pressirostres, 47.
Pride, 1.
Pristiurus, 24.
Procellaria, 57.
Procellariidæ, 57.
Progne, 31.
Psophia, 45.
Psophiidæ, 45.
Ptarmigan, 44.
Pteroclidæ, 43.
Pterocyanea, 54.
Puffin, 61.
Puffinus, 57.
Purre, 48.
Putorius, 70.
Pycnonotus, 36.
Pygmy Curlew, 48.
Pygopodes, 60.
Pyrgita, 39.
Pyrrhocorax, 43.
Pyrrhula, 39.

Quail, 44.
Querquedula, 54.

Rabbit, 65.
Rabbit-fish, 25.
Raia, 21.
Raiidæ, 21.

Rail, 46.
Rainbow Wrasse, 10.
Rain-fowl, 29.
Rallidæ, 46.
Rallus, 46.
Rana, 26.
Raniceps, 9.
Ranidæ, 26.
Raptores, 61.
Rasores, 43.
Rat, 65.
Raven, 42.
Ray, 22.
Razorback, 68.
Razorbill, 61.
Recurvirostra, 50.
Red Bream, 18.
Redbreast, 35.
Red Deer, 68.
Red Grouse, 44.
Red Mullet, 19.
Redpoll, 40.
Redshank, 49.
Redstart, 35.
Redwing, 36.
Red-winged Starling, 42.
Reed-Warbler, 34.
Reeve, 49.
Regalecus, 12.
Regulus, 35.
Remora, 15.
Reptilia, 27.
Rhina, 23.
Rhinolophus, 67.
Rhodostethia, 59.
Rhombus, 6.
Rhynchaspis, 54.
Ribbon-fish, 12.
Ring-Dove, 43.
Ringed Plover, 47.
Ring-Ouzel, 36.

Rissa, 59.
Roach, 3.
Robin, 35.
Rock-Cook, 10.
Rock-Dove, 43.
Rock-fish, 13.
Rockling, 8, 9.
Rock-Mullet, 17.
Rodentia, 65.
Roebuck, 68.
Rogenia, 2.
Roller, 30.
Rook, 42.
Rorqual, 68.
Rose-coloured Starling, 42.
Rosores, 65.
Rotche, 61.
Rubecula, 35.
Rudd, 3.
Ruff, 49.
Ruffe, 19.
Ruminantia, 68.
Ruticilla, 35.

Sail-fluke, 7.
Salamandridæ, 26.
Salicaria, 34.
Salmo, 5.
Salmon, 5.
Salmonidæ, 5.
Salmon-peel, 5.
Sand-Eel, 8.
Sanderling, 48.
Sand-Grouse, 43.
Sand-Lizard, 27.
Sand-Martin, 31.
Sandnecker, 6.
Sandpiper, 49.
Sand-Smelt, 11.
Sardine, 2.
Sauria, 27.
Saury Pike, 4.
Saxicola, 36.

Scabbard-fish, 16.
Scad, 14.
Scald-fish, 7.
Scansores, 29, 32.
Scaup Duck, 55.
Schedophilus, 16.
Schœnicola, 40.
Sciæna, 17.
Sciænidæ, 17.
Sciuridæ, 66.
Sciurus, 66.
Sclerodermi, 21.
Scolecophagus, 42.
Scolopacidæ, 48.
Scolopax, 50.
Scomber, 15.
Scombresocidæ, 4.
Scombresox, 4.
Scombridæ, 15.
Scopelidæ, 6.
Scopelus, 6.
Scops, 64.
Scorpænidæ, 18.
Scoter, 56.
Scraber, 61.
Scylliidæ, 24.
Scyllium, 24.
Sea-Adder, 20.
Sea-Ape, 24.
Sea-Bream, 16.
Sea-Calf, 70.
Sea-Cat, 12.
Sea-Cow, 70.
Sea-Devil, 13, 22.
Sea-Fox, 24.
Sea-Hog, 69.
Sea-Horse, 20.
Seal, 70.
Sea-Loche, 8.
Sea-mew, 58.
Sea-Owl, 13.
Sea-Parrot, 61.
Sea-Perch, 19.
Sea-Pie, 48.

INDEX.

Sea-Scorpion, 18.
Sea-Snail, 13.
Sea-Snipe, 48.
Sea-Swallow, 59.
Sea-Trout, 5.
Sea-Unicorn, 68.
Sea-Wolf, 12.
Sebastes, 18.
Sedge-Warbler, 34.
Selache, 24.
Selachoidei, 23.
Selenodontia, 68.
Serin, 40.
Serinus, 40.
Serranus, 19.
Sewen, 5.
Shad, 2.
Shag, 57.
Shanny, 12.
Shark, 23.
Shearwater, 57.
Sheldrake, 54.
Shore-Lark, 41.
Shoveller, 54.
Shrew, 67.
Shrew-Mouse, 67.
Shrike, 33.
Sibilatrix, 34.
Siphonostoma, 20.
Siskin, 39.
Sitta, 32.
Skate, 21.
Skipper, 4.
Skua, 58.
Skulpin, 14.
Sky-Lark, 41.
Slow-worm, 28.
Smear-Dab, 7.
Smelt, 5.
Smew, 56.
Smolt, 5.
Smooth Hound, 25.
Snake, 27.

Snake-bird, 57.
Snig-Eel, 2.
Snipe, 50.
Snow-Bunting, 40.
Snowy Owl, 64.
Solan Goose, 56.
Sole, 7.
Solea, 7.
Solenette, 7.
Somateria, 56.
Sorex, 67.
Soricidæ, 67.
Sparidæ, 18.
Sparrow, 39.
Sparrow-Hawk, 62.
Spatula, 54.
Sperm-Whale, 68.
Sphargis, 28.
Sphyrna, 25.
Spinachia, 20.
Spinacidæ, 23.
Spinax, 23.
Spinous Shark, 23.
Spiza, 40.
Spoonbill, 51.
Spotted Crake, 46.
Sprat, 2.
Spur-winged Goose, 53.
Squacco Heron, 52.
Squalus, 24.
Squatarola, 47.
Squatina, 23.
Squatinidæ, 23.
Squirrel, 66.
Stag, 68.
Stare, 41.
Starling, 41.
Starna, 44.
Steganopodes, 56.
Stelleria, 55.
Stercorarius, 58.

Sterna, 59.
Sternoptychidæ, 6.
Sternula, 59.
Stichæus, 12.
Stickleback, 20.
Stilt, 50.
Sting-fish, 17, 18.
Sting-Ray, 22.
Stint, 48.
Stoat, 70.
Stock-Dove, 43.
Stone-Basse, 17, 19.
Stonechat, 35.
Stone-Curlew, 48.
Stork, 51.
Storm-Petrel, 57.
Strepsilas, 47.
Strigidæ, 64.
Strix, 65.
Strobilophaga, 39.
Stromateidæ, 16.
Sturgeon, 25.
Sturnella, 42.
Sturnidæ, 41.
Sturnus, 41.
Stylochelidon, 59.
Sucker, 11.
Sucking-fish, 15.
Sula, 56.
Summer Curlew, 50.
Summer Duck, 55.
Summer Snipe, 48.
Sun-fish, 16, 21, 24.
Surmullet, 19.
Surnia, 64.
Swallow, 31.
Swallow-tailed Kite, 62.
Swan, 53.

Swift, 31.
Swordfish, 14.
Sylbeocyclus, 60.
Sylvia, 33.
Sylviidæ, 33.
Syndactyli, 30.
Syngnathidæ, 20.
Syngnathus, 20.
Synotus, 66.
Syrrhaptes, 43.

Tachybaptes, 60.
Tachycineta, 31.
Tadorna, 54.
Talpa, 67.
Talpidæ, 67.
Tantalidæ, 51.
Teal, 54.
Teleostei, 2.
Tench, 4.
Tenuirostres, 32.
Tern, 59.
Testudinata, 28.
Testudinidæ, 28.
Testudo, 28.
Tetrao, 44.
Tetraonidæ, 44.
Tetrodon, 21.
Thalassidroma, 57.
Thornback, 22.
Thremmaphilus, 42.
Thresher, 24.
Thrush, 36.
Thymallus, 5.
Thynnus, 15.
Tichodroma, 32.
Tinca, 4.
Tinnunculus, 63.
Tit, 38.
Titlark, 37.
Titmouse, 38.
Toad, 26.

Tompot, 12.
Tope, 25.
Topknot, 7.
Torgoch, 5.
Torpedinidæ, 23.
Torpedo, 23.
Torquilla, 30.
Torsk, 9.
Tortoise, 28.
Totanus, 49.
Totipalmatæ, 56.
Trachinidæ, 17.
Trachinus, 17.
Trachurus, 14.
Trachypteridæ, 12.
Trachypterus, 12.
Trichiuridæ, 16.
Trichiurus, 16.
Trigla, 17.
Triglidæ, 17.
Tringa, 48.
Tringoides, 49.
Triton, 26.
Troglodytes, 38.
Troglodytidæ, 38.
Tropidonotus, 27.
Trout, 5.
Trumpeter, 45.
Trumpet-fish, 11.
Trygon, 22.
Trygonidæ, 22.
Tryngites, 49.
Tub, 17.
Tubinares, 57.
Tunny, 15.
Turbot, 6.
Turdidæ, 36.
Turdus, 36.
Turnix, 44.
Turnstone, 47.
Turtle, 28.
Turtle-Dove, 43.
Turtur, 43.

Tusk, 9.
Twite, 40.

Ungulata, 68.
Upupa, 30.
Upupidæ, 30.
Urchin, 67.
Uria, 61.
Urodela, 26.
Utamania, 61.

Vaagmaer, 12.
Vagellus, 57.
Vanellus, 47.
Vendace, 5.
Vespertilio, 66.
Vespertilionidæ, 66.
Vesperugo, 67.
Viper, 27.
Vipera, 27.
Vireo, 33.
Vireosylvia, 33.
Virginian Quail, 44.
Vole, 65.
Volitores, 30.
Volucres, 29, 30, 32, 43.
Vulpes, 71.
Vulture, 61.
Vulturidæ, 61.

Wagtail, 37.
Wall-creeper, 32.
Walrus, 70.
Want, 67.
Warbler, 34.
Water-Hen, 46.
Water-Ouzel, 37.
Water-Rat, 65.
Water-Shrew, 67.
Water-Vole, 65.
Weasel, 70.

INDEX.

Weever, 17.
Whale, 68.
Wheatear, 36.
Whiff, 7.
Whimbrel, 50.
Whinchat, 35.
Whistler, 8.
White, 5.
Whitebait, 2.
White-fish, 69.
White Nun, 56.
White Shark, 24.
Whitethroat, 33.
White Whale, 69.
Whiting, 9.
Whiting-pout, 9.
Whooper, 53.
Wide-gab, 13.
Wigeon, 54.
Wild Oat, 71.

Wild Duck, 54.
Wild Goose, 53.
Wild Swan, 53.
Willock, 61.
Willow-Wren, 34.
Windhover, 63.
Winnard, 36.
Wolf-fish, 12.
Woodchat, 33.
Woodcock, 50.
Wood-Lark, 41.
Wood-Mouse, 65.
Woodpecker, 29.
Wood-Pigeon, 43.
Wood-Sandpiper, 49.
Wood-Wren, 34.
Wrasse, 10.
Wren, 38.
Wryneck, 30.

Xema, 59.
Xiphias, 14.
Xiphiidæ, 14.
Xylocota, 50.

Yellow-Hammer, 40.
Yellowshank, 49.
Yunx, 30.

Zapornia, 46.
Zeugopterus, 7.
Zeus, 16.
Ziphius, 69.
Zoarces, 12.
Zonotrichia, 41.
Zootoca, 28.
Zygæna, 25.
Zygodactyli, 29, 32.

THE END.

www.ingramcontent.com/pod-product-compliance
Lightning Source LLC
Chambersburg PA
CBHW031604110426
42742CB00037B/1101